Translation and Multilingual Natural Language Processing

Chief Editor: Oliver Čulo (Johannes Gutenberg-Universität Mainz)
Consulting Editors: Silvia Hansen-Schirra (Johannes Gutenberg-Universität Mainz), Reinhard Rapp (Johannes Gutenberg-Universität Mainz)

In this series:

ISSN: 2364-8899

Eyetracking and Applied Linguistics

Edited by

Silvia Hansen-Schirra

Sambor Grucza

Silvia Hansen-Schirra & Sambor Grucza (eds.). 2016. *Eyetracking and Applied Linguistics* (Translation and Multilingual Natural Language Processing 2). Berlin: Language Science Press.

This title can be downloaded at:
http://langsci-press.org//catalog/book/108
© 2016, the authors

ISBN: 978-3-944675-98-5 (Digital)
      978-3-946234-65-4 (Hardcover)
      978-3-946234-69-2 (Softcover)
      978-1-537653-20-4 (Softcover US)
ISSN: 2364-8899
DOI:10.17169/langsci.b108.230

Cover and concept of design: Ulrike Harbort
Typesetting: Oliver Čulo, Sebastian Nordhoff, Florian Stuhlmann
Proofreading: Alec Shaw, Andreas Hölzl, Anelia Stefanova, Anne Kilgus, Benedikt Singpiel, Eitan Grossmann, Gabrielle Hodge, Georgy Krasovitskiy, Jean Nitzke, Joseph de Veaugh, Martin Haspelmath, Rachele De Felice, Stathis Selimis, Viola Wiegand
Fonts: Linux Libertine, Arimo, DejaVu Sans Mono, Aozora Mincho
Typesetting software: XƎLᴬTEX

Language Science Press
Habelschwerdter Allee 45
14195 Berlin, Germany
langsci-press.org
Storage and cataloguing done by FU Berlin

Contents

Contents

Indexes   **187**

Chapter 1

Eyetracking and Applied Linguistics

Silvia Hansen-Schirra

Johannes Gutenberg University of Mainz in Germersheim

Sambor Grucza

University of Warsaw

1 Introduction

Eyetracking has become a powerful tool in scientific research and has finally found its way into disciplines such as Applied Linguistics and Translation Studies, paving the way for new insights and challenges in these fields. The aim of the first International Conference on Eyetracking and Applied Linguistics (ICEAL) was to bring together researchers who use eyetracking to empirically answer their research questions. It was intended to bridge the gaps between Applied Linguistics, Translation Studies, Cognitive Science and Computational Linguistics on the one hand and to further encourage innovative research methodologies and data triangulation on the other hand. Despite their inherent common interests, methodological exchange between these disciplines is rare. Thus, the conference served as a platform for interdisciplinary exchange and to exploit synergy effects. This proceedings volume focusses on the major topics that emerged during the aforementioned conference: audiovisual translation, post-editing as well as comprehensibility and usability. Eyetracking methodology is employed to empirically investigate all of said topics.

The first part of the volume is dedicated to empirical studies in audiovisual translation. The volume begins with a contribution by Wendy Fox, who tests the efficiency of integrated titles vs. traditional subtitles for the language pair English-German. For the creation of the integrated titles, she considers placement and design, which are proven to have an effect on reading time of the

Silvia Hansen-Schirra & Sambor Grucza. 2016. Eyetracking and Applied Linguistics. In Silvia Hansen-Schirra & Sambor Grucza (eds.), *Eyetracking and Applied Linguistics*, 1–4. Berlin: Language Science Press. DOI:10.17169/langsci.b108.232

titles and perception of the image. The eyetracking data show that split attention improves in favour of a more undistracted gaze behaviour of the image. Minako O'Hagan & Ryoko Sasamoto present an eyetracking study on Japanese impact captions intended to have an entertaining effect from the perspective of the TV producers. They contrast the differing results, which show unconscious eye movements vs. interviews focussing on the conscious impression of the subjects. As a result, the limitations and advantages of the research question as well as the methodology are discussed. Finally, Juha Lång introduces two experiments investigating the degree of information acquisition from a subtitled television documentary for the language pair Russian-Finnish. The eyetracking data is triangulated with comprehension tests involving subject groups with different language skills. The author concludes with presenting the parallel processing of two information channels, i.e. narration and subtitles, as well as the efficiency of the subtitles and their potential for distraction.

The second part of this volume deals with post-editing of machine translation output. Within this context, Jean Nitzke focusses on monolingual post-editing for English-German machine translation. She investigates the quality of the final translations as well as the research patterns of the post-editors on the basis of the eyetracking data. She concludes with an evaluation of typical error types and the effort needed to accomplish the monolingual post-editing tasks. Within the same realm, Fabio Alves and colleagues analyse the cognitive effort exerted during post-editing from a relevance-theoretical perspective. The concepts of conceptual and procedural encoding are used for the empirical operationalization of the eyetracking results. These reveal the efficiency of interactive post-editing in contrast to other translation tasks and promote this type of computer-aided translation.

Finally, this volume addresses questions of comprehensibility and usability. Christoph Rösener reports on the experiences of creating a usability lab with eyetracking technology. He discusses general challenges and obstacles as well as specific equipment issues in concrete terms. He exemplifies his considerations by introducing the design of the usability laboratory at Flensburg University of Applied Sciences. Sascha Wolfer tackles the topic of comprehensibility in Text Linguistics. In his eyetracking study, he contrasts German jurisdictional texts with reformulations intended to be more comprehensible with respect to nominalisations. The eyetracking corpus is investigated in terms of reading times, regression paths as well as statistical probability assessments. While the reformulations can also be regarded within the paradigm of intralingual translation, the eyetracking data focus on the readability and processing effort for the given text type and thus on empirical research in Applied Linguistics in general.

While the studies contained in this volume draw from a variety of objectives and various areas of overlaps between Applied Linguistics, Translation Studies and Cognitive Science, they all agree on eyetracking as an appropriate methodology in empirical research. However, it should be emphasised that the volume is by no means exhaustive with regard to this research area. Further crossfertilisation is not only desirable, but almost mandatory in order to tackle future tasks and endeavours, and the ICEAL conference series remains committed to bringing these fields even closer together.

As a final remark, we would like to thank everyone who participated in making the ICEAL conference series as well as this volume possible. The authors of the individual articles put a lot of time and effort into their papers, and it was a pleasure working with them. We are also deeply indebted to our anonymous reviewers for their thorough and thought-provoking work, which decisively contributed to the quality of this volume.

Silvia Hansen-Schirra & Sambor Grucza

Chapter 2

Integrated titles: An improved viewing experience?

Wendy Fox

Johannes Gutenberg University of Mainz in Germersheim

While there are a few examples of (sub)titles placed individually in the image as a means of translation of an additional language into the film's main language, this practice has not yet been used to commercially translate a complete film for a foreign target audience. Using eye tracking data, this study examines to what extent the placement and design of (sub)titles affect reading time and the visual perception of the image. The applied placement strategies were based on the undistracted focus points of 14 English native participants and image composition principles from film studies. Additional 31 German participants with little or no knowledge of English watched the English film with traditional subtitles or integrated titles. The results of the eye tracking data analysis indicate that, while reaction time (time to first fixation) increases, the reading time (total visit duration) for integrated titles decreases, the viewers are less likely to focus on the title area before the title appears and their focus resembles the undistracted gaze behaviour of the native participants to a much greater degree. Additionally, the split attention between image and title shifts towards the image. Integrated titles appear to motivate the viewer to return to the focal points faster and spend more time exploring the image in between titles. Their placement allows for shorter saccades and thereby decreases the time in which no visual information is obtained.

1 Introduction

Historically a dubbing country[1], Germany is not well-known for subtitled productions. However, while dubbing is obviously predominant in Germany and other neighbouring countries with a similar language-related history and a sufficiently large target audience, more and more German viewers prefer the original

---

[1] For the history of dubbing in Germany, refer to http://www.sprechersprecher.de/blog/die-geschichte-der-film-synchronisation-in-deutschland [30.12.2014, in German].

Wendy Fox. 2016. Integrated titles: An improved viewing experience? In Silvia Hansen-Schirra & Sambor Grucza (eds.), *Eyetracking and Applied Linguistics*, 5–30. Berlin: Language Science Press. DOI:10.17169/langsci.b108.233

versions of English film productions.[2] Fans of series such as *Game of Thrones* (HBO, USA/UK 2011-) or *The Big Bang Theory* (CBS, USA 2007-) yearn for every new episode and many do not want to wait for the German dubbed version. Combined with the desire for a more authentic film experience, many German viewers prefer original and subtitled versions of their favourite show.[3]

Traditional subtitling can be seen as a strong intrusion into the original image composition that may disrupt or even destroy the director's intended shot composition and focal points. But isn't the carefully composed interplay of image and sound what makes film "the most popular art form" (Mercado 2010: 35) of today's entertainment landscape? Long saccades between focal points and subtitles affect the viewer's information intake and in particular the German audience, who are not used to subtitles, seems to prefer to wait for the next subtitle instead of looking back up again.[4] Furthermore, not only the placement, but also the overall design of traditional subtitles can disturb the image composition – for instance titles with a weak contrast, inappropriate typeface or irritating colour system. So should it not, despite the translation process, be possible to preserve both image and sound as far as possible by designing and placing subtitles differently? Today's numerous artistic and technical possibilities combined with the immense amount of work that goes into the visual aspects of a film, taking into account not only special effects, but also typefaces, opening credits and text-image compositions, should enable producers to do so. A further development of existing subtitling guidelines would not only express respect towards the original film version but also the translator's work.

The present study is based on Just and Carpenter's strong eye-mind hypothesis, which states that "there is no appreciable lag between what is fixated and what is processed" (1980: 331). Caffrey notes a recent increase in "output from researchers into the perception of translated AV content employing data generated with eye trackers" (2009: 4), mentioning Moran (2008) and Perego & Del

---

[2] This is reflected in the increasing number of screenings of original versions in German cinemas (see for example http://www.koeln.de/kino/ov-filme [16.12.2014, in German] and http://against-dubbing.com/de/ovkinos/ [16.12.2014, in German]), especially since the introduction of digital film, changing from 35mm film to digital projection. This allowed for a considerably easier and more cost-efficient process for film distributors (see http://www.dw.de/der-35mm-film-stirbt-aus-kino-wird-digital/a-17013764 [16.12.2014, in German]).

[3] This assumption is supported by the increasing number of German internet forums that centre around creating and providing fansubs – subtitles created by fans – for download: subcentral.de with approximately 134 new posts per day, subtitles.de, tv4user.de and opensubtitles.org [30.12.2014].

[4] This is indicated by the high amount of fixations in the subtitle area before the subtitle actually appears, as explained in Figure 8 in §4.1

Missier (2008). Cognitive psychologists such as d'Ydewalle, Van Rensbergen & Pollet (1985), Koolstra, van der Voort & d'Ydewalle (1999) and d'Ydewalle & De Bruycker (2007) analysed fixation-based eye tracking data such as the perception of one- and two-liners, while Kruger, Hefer & Matthew (2013) discuss the impact of subtitles on the cognitive load and support their hypotheses with eye tracking data. Most research on new forms of subtitles relates to fan-produced subtitles (Nornes 1999; Ferrer Simó 2005; Pérez Gonzáles 2007; Cintas & Sánchez 2006; Orrego-Carmona 2014) and only a few focus on commercially oriented subtitles (Díaz Cintas 2005; Caffrey 2009). Caffrey (2009) and McClarty (2012; 2013b,a) present two of the more recent eye tracking-based studies on innovative subtitling methods. There are already several terms that attempt to grasp these new subtitling concepts and designs: "abusive subtitles" (Nornes 1999, 2004) describes the experimental use of subtitles in regard to both graphical and linguistic aspects while the terms "hybrid" (Cintas & Sánchez 2006) and "creative" (McClarty 2012) subtitles focus on the overall presentation and are presented in opposition to traditionally placed and designed subtitles. Even though these terms cover many of the differences between traditional subtitles and more recent concepts, they do not seem to apply to the titles used in Fox (2012) and the present study as they might still refer to subtitles being automatically placed in the bottom (or top) area of the screen. Therefore, the term "integrated titles" (Fox 2012) was used, referring to titles being integrated[5] into the shot composition. At the same time, this term describes the novelty of the present study: So far, there have been no eye tracking studies of German integrated titles[6] or – as Germany is traditionally a dubbing country – much research on subtitling in general. Additionally, no eye tracking study has been conducted on the aesthetics and perception of subtitles combined with attempts to draft a new, updated set of guidelines for recent subtitling concepts.

While there are only a few examples of English productions that use individually placed titles – for instance *Man on Fire* (Twentieth Century Fox, USA/UK 2004), *Heroes* (NBC, USA 2006-2010) and *Slumdog Millionaire* (Warner Bros., USA/UK 2008) – there are even fewer examples of recreations of these kinds of "text inserts" (Molerov 2012) and titles for the German version, e.g. the series *Sherlock* (BBC/Hartswood Films 2010-) and *Stark Trek Into Darkness* (Paramount Pictures, USA 2013). Creatively placed titles such as in *Heroes* and *Man on Fire* were removed during the translation process into German and traditional subtitles accompanied the dubbed version.

---

[5] Inspired by Bayram & Bayraktar (2012) who described "text information [that is placed] directly into the picture" [82] as "integrated formats".

[6] For studies on integrated titles in English, see McClarty (2013a) and Brown et al. (2015).

This research is relevant not only because of the increasing use of integrated titles in English film productions but also because of the fact that "even though these translation and accessibility services only account for 0.1% – 1% of the budget of an average film production (Lambourne 2012), over half of the revenue of, for example, both top-grossing and award-winning Hollywood films comes from foreign territories" (Romero-Fresco 2013: 202). Therefore, it is only in the interest of film producers to take a critical look at the perception of the translated version of their film and studies on more content- and image-related ways of audiovisual translation might be helpful in motivating this shift. An alternative placement of titles might allow for a positive split attention towards the image and therefore enable a viewing behaviour more similar to that of the native audience and closer to the intended focal points, while taking into consideration both image composition and typographic identity of the film.

A previous pilot study (Fox 2012) examining the first episode of the British TV series *Being Human* (BBC/Touchpaper, UK 2008-; so far without official German subtitles or dubbing) evaluated whether integrated titles improve understanding without interfering with the composition and aesthetics of the episode. In a basic three-step-experiment, the advantages and disadvantages of integrated titles were analysed by recording the eye movements of 45 participants. The results indicated that the reduced time spent on (long) saccadic eye movements gives viewers more time to focus on the image and makes it easier for them to link the titles to the plot. Moreover, the film material was perceived as more aesthetic and closer to the original version.

The present eye tracking study addresses whether the individual placement and design of (sub)titles affect the viewer's reading time, the time spent exploring the image (rather than waiting for the next title) as well as the overall viewing experience, including the time spent on the intended focal points and the split attention between image and (sub)title. Additional thought was given to indicating speech direction and rate as well as speaker position. While the study also included the creation and translation of the necessary subtitles and integrated titles, the present article focuses on the eye tracking experiment and its results. Pablo Romero-Fresco gave his permission to use his short documentary *Joining the Dots* (UK 2012) and agreed to discuss his image system and shot compositions as a first step to creating the integrated titles. These were based on adjusted traditional guidelines, guidelines created during previous work (Fox 2012) and a first sketch of the modular guidelines that are presented in Fox (2015). 14 English native participants watched the film without subtitles in order to define the most common focus points[7] and provide reference data. 15 native speakers of German with little or no knowledge of English[8] watched the film with traditional subtitles and an additional 16 German native-speakers with little or no knowledge of English[9] watched the film with integrated titles. The gaze behaviour of the German participants was analysed in regard to reaction times (time to first fixation), reading times (total visit duration) and general visual attention distribution between image and (sub)title.

Based on the pilot study (Fox 2012), expected results are decreased reading times and a gaze behaviour more similar to that of the English native speakers. It is to be assumed that the reaction time for integrated titles is slightly longer than for traditional titles. Due to the individual placement of the titles, the distance between focal point and title is on average smaller and the viewer would therefore gain more time to explore the image and focus on the focal points. Overall, expectations are that integrated titles will have a positive effect on both the aesthetic viewing experience of the audience and the split-attention between image and title, as integrated titles appear to motivate the viewer to return to the main focal point faster and spend more time exploring the image in between titles.

2 Setup

2.1 Film

Joining the Dots is a short documentary by Pablo Romero-Fresco, screened for the first time in 2012.[10] The documentary shows an interview with Trevor Franklin who went blind at the age of 60. He speaks about his experiences and how he handles the disability. The main topic of the documentary is accessibility for the blind, focusing on television and theatre. In an interview with Pablo Romero-Fresco, the image system, compositions and key elements in the various scenes were defined and possible placements and designs discussed. Due to its docu-

---

[7] Note that, while the 'focal points' refer to the intended focus created by the director using image composition and technical elements, the 'focus points' are areas fixated by the majority of the participants.

[8] According to the participants' own statements.

[9] According to the participants' own statements.

[10] For further information on *Joining the Dots*, see http://www.jostrans.org/issue20/intromero. php [28.10.2014].

Figure 1: Frontal shots of the interviewees in Joining the Dots (UK 2012)

Figure 2: Static scenes with evenly balanced primary and secondary areas (*Joining the Dots*, UK 2012)

mental character, *Joining the Dots* offers a simple image system[11] and clearly structured shot compositions. Frontal shots of the persons being interviewed are predominant (see Figure 1) while further scenes introduce important places in Trevor's life such as the theatre or his home. The interview situations and several other rather static scenes (see Figure 2) are well suited for integrated titles as the primary and secondary areas are quite clear and the secondary area offers enough space for the titles. Due to their rather static character, there is no immense risk of important elements being covered by the titles.

The definition of primary and secondary areas is based on the analysis of the image composition and the resulting focal points in the image. According to Mercado, "focal points refer to the center of interest in a composition, the area where the viewer's gaze will gravitate to because of the arrangement of all the

---

[11] For a definition of "image system" see Mercado (2010: 21): "[...] refers to the use of recurrent images and compositions in a film to add layers of meaning to a narrative. ...Because the experience of watching a film relies so much on the use of images ([...]), most films have an image system at work at some level, whether the filmmaker intends to have one or not." It is important to distinguish between the image system of a film and the individual "shot compositions" of a scene.

visual elements in the frame." (2010: 11) Thus, the combination of several technical aspects such as the used lenses that define the sharp areas in the image automatically attracts the viewer's gaze to where the director wants it to be. These are seen as primary areas and should not be covered by text. Other concepts that can help to define primary and secondary areas and "isolate the subject within the frame" (2010: 35) are the "rule of thirds" (2010: 7), "Hitchcock's rule", "balanced/unbalanced compositions" and the overall "visual weight" (2010: 8) of elements in the shot composition. The eye tracking recordings with the English native-speakers confirmed this theory and allowed for the distribution based on the eye tracking data. Figure 3 shows an example of a heat map of the focus points of the English native participants and the corresponding definition of the primary and secondary areas.

Aside from these rather static image compositions, *Joining the Dots* includes several recurring compositions. Images with mainly blurred or fast moving elements underline the interviewee's statements, for example as Trevor speaks about the progressing loss of his sight (see Figure 4).

The German subtitles were created according to the traditional guidelines described by Ivarsson & Carroll (1998) and Karamitroglou (1998). The integrated titles consisted of the same translation but were modified according to the discussion of traditional guidelines in Fox (2012). These modifications included more individual fade durations and a much scarcer use of the three dots at the end of a title. For aesthetical reasons, no commas were placed at the end of a title and dialogs were not combined in the same title for the sake of improved speaker identification. No italics were used to indicate a speaker outside the shot as it is very clear throughout the whole documentation whether the speaker is visible in the current shot or not. Even though this version of *Joining the Dots* is intended for a hearing audience and the modifications are based on the assumption that

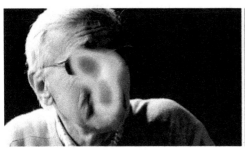 

Figure 3: Fixation points of English natives (left) and resulting primary/secondary areas (*Joining the Dots*, UK 2012)

Figure 4: Scenes that support the overall atmosphere in *Joining the Dots* (UK 2012)

the audience can connect the visible with the audible content, adjustments such as the individual placement might already provide additional information for the hearing-impaired. For a more accessible translation, useful visual elements need to be re-evaluated and adjusted to the needs of the respective target group.

2.2 Placement

As the interviews are the main element of the documentary, it was decided not to place every title individually but rather to define rough areas of title placement for the three interviewees. Therefore, Trevor's titles are displayed in the right half of the image as he tends to look to the right. The titles for Joan Greening and Mags Silbery are displayed on the left half as they tend to look to the left. These positions were also supported by the positions of the captions with their names (see Figure 1) and the secondary areas in the corresponding shot compositions. Figure 5 illustrates how the secondary areas often allow for a more even and stronger contrast. Keeping the positions of the placements to a minimum, even if the shot composition changes noticeably, might allow for more accessible adjustment, for instance for a hearing-impaired or deaf audience. For such an audience, with a possibly greater need for additional visual information, speaker-related positions allow for faster identification of the speaker, even if he or she is not visible on the screen. Colour is another possibility to make identification easier, even though it is not always easy to come up with a suitable colour concept for a film that works throughout the whole story.

Figure 5: Roughly defined areas for Trevor (to the right of the speaker) and Mags (to the left of the speaker; *Joining the Dots*, UK 2012)

2.3 Typography

The original version of *Joining the Dots* used two typefaces: Today's MS Office standard typeface *Calibri*[12] to display names (see Figure 1) and *Slab Serif*[13] for the film title. The closing credits are a mixture of both typefaces. The title design for *Joining the Dots* was based on a detailed interview with the director Pablo Romero-Fresco and the analysis of the existing examples of integrated titles and creative solutions. After various typographic tests with typefaces and spatial effects, the typeface *Gill Sans* was chosen for the translation of the film title. The typeface was not only chosen for its appearance but also for the graphic designer behind it: Eric Gill[14], an important English sculptor, typographer and graphic designer. The very British elements and characteristics of the documentary should also be visible in the typeface, and as "Gill Sans [is] part of the British visual heritage just like the Union Jack and the safety pin" (Archer 2007), it met this criterion. Besides the historic reference to the United Kingdom, *Gill Sans Bold* is suitable as a screen typeface due to its high readability – the bold style's higher stroke weight ensures a good contrast and the clear design is unlikely to distract from the content. The film title itself was not to be replaced during translation but rather to be accompanied by a subtitle. To underline the individuality of the project but also the manual translation act – a little reminder of the fact that a translator was at work and, at least for this project, even part of the film production –, the handwritten typeface *Dakota*[15] was chosen for this subtitle.

---

[12] For further information on the typeface *Calibri*, see http://www.lucasfonts.com/case-studies/calibri-consolas/ [29.12.2014].

[13] For further information on the typeface *Slab Serif*, see http://www.linotype.com/3493/introduction.html [29.12.2014].

[14] For further information on Eric Gill, see http://www.ericgill.org.uk/Gill/ [05.12.2014].

[15] For further information on the typeface *Dakota*, see https://www.vletter.com/downloads/dakota-font-download-free.html [17.12.2014].

2.4 Participants

Of the 45 participants, 14 were native speakers of English between the age of 18 and 45 who study at the FTSK[16] and watched the original version of *Joining the Dots*. As film audiences are usually not homogenous groups, no other characteristics besides native language and eye sight were determined. Each participant claimed to have normal or corrected-to-normal vision. Thirty-one participants were German native speakers who stated that they rely on German subtitles to understand English films. As using subtitles is a personal decision based on the viewer's self-assessment and not his or her factual knowledge of the foreign language (and on availability), the actual level of the participants' English was not determined. Of these participants with German as their native language, 15 randomly chosen participants watched *Joining the Dots* with traditional subtitles in German. The other 16 German participants watched the film with the integrated titles. None of the participants had seen the film before.

3 Method

The aim of the present study was to evaluate the participants' resulting visual attention and overall aesthetic experience with integrated titles compared to traditional subtitles. Visual attention can be measured by examining the participants' gaze behaviour, expressed in fixations and saccades. These eye movements can be recorded with an eye tracker,[17] in this case the Tobii TX300. Even though the human eye is quite simplistic in its physical structure, it is not a mere "sensor" (Joos, Rötting & Velichkovsky 2002: 1) and responsible for the "exploration" of the surroundings but also part of communicative interaction and indicates cognitive processes. The strong eye-mind hypothesis by Just & Carpenter (1980) states that eye movements are correlates of mental processing. The different kinds of observed eye movements are divided into various categories. Fixations and saccades are particularly relevant for the analysis of eye movements. During fixations, a specific point in space – the fixation point – is at the centre of visual attention. The typical mean duration of a fixation is between 200 and 300 ms with the minimal fixation duration being around 100 ms (Rayner 1998:

---

[16] Abbreviation for "Fachbereich Translations-, Sprach- und Kulturwissenschaft", the "Faculty of Translation Studies, Linguistics and Cultural Studies" in Germersheim and part of the Johannes Gutenberg University of Mainz.

[17] For a short overview on eye tracking history, refer to http://www.uxbooth.com/blog/a-brief-history-of-eye-tracking/ [21.11.2014, in German] and http://www.cs.hs-rm.de/~linn/fachsem0809/eyetracking/Eye_Tracking.pdf [21.11.2014, in German].

373; Flothow 2009: 2). Usually, fixations are considerably longer, especially during reading (see Rayner 1998; Lykke Jakobsen & Jensen 2008). Saccades are the movements between the fixation points, describing the movement of the eye from one point to another. These ballistic eye movements are especially abrupt – according to Joos, Helmert & Pannasch (2005: 17), the latency is around 150 to 200 ms – and with speeds up to 1000°/s, they are so fast that the eye cannot absorb or process any information (Flothow 2009: 4). Information absorbed during fixations, however, is processed during the following saccades (Kowler 2006: 6), usually preventing information loss and deficits. In the present study, fixations and saccades are analysed as indicators of the participants' focus of attention. The following indicators of visual attention and the viewing experience during film are used in the present study:

- **Reading time:** The reading time is measured in seconds from the first to the last fixation on a (sub)title. The data evaluation in Fox (2012) already indicated a decreased reading time compared to traditional subtitles. The viewer seemed to re-read integrated titles less often and was more motivated to return to the focal points in the image.

- **Correspondence to undistracted focus[18]:** To allow for a viewing experience that is close to that of a native audience, the gaze behaviour should be as similar as possible and the same main focus points should be fixated.

- **Reaction time:** The time between when the (sub)title fades in and the first fixation by the viewer, measured as the time to first fixation in the area. If this time is increased considerably by integrated titles, this could be a counterargument for individual placement. As this seems to be the main concern of critics of integrated titles, the reaction times of traditional subtitles and integrated titles should be compared and their difference discussed.

- **Aesthetic experience:** The participants for the integrated titles will be asked to fill in a questionnaire on their aesthetic experience and rate it compared to traditional subtitles.

Based on the earlier pilot study and review, the following hypotheses on integrated titles (IT) and traditional titles (TS) emerged:

---

[18] The 'undistracted focus' refers to the viewing behaviour of the English native participants that watched the film without subtitles.

Visual attention (based on eye tracking data):

- Hypothesis 1: The reading time of IT is shorter than for TS.

- Hypothesis 2: The IT participants experience a positive split attention.[19]

- Hypothesis 3: The IT participants are more likely to fixate the same focus points as the native participants.

- Hypothesis 4: The time to first fixation of the IT participants is higher than that of the TS participants.

Aesthetical experience (based on questionnaire):

- Hypothesis 5: The IT participants experience a higher information intake.

- Hypothesis 6: The integrated titles are ranked as more aesthetic.

In this study, these hypotheses are tested and discussed based on the collected eye tracking and questionnaire data. Every recording session started with the participant being introduced to the eye tracking lab and the eye tracker. No warm up tasks were performed and the artificial lighting in the window-less laboratory room provided stable conditions. The participant watched the episode without any prior knowledge of the topic or the aim of the experiment. The German native speakers who watched the version with the integrated titles then filled in a questionnaire designed to cover subjective information flow and aesthetics of the titles. To collect the data on visual attention, the areas including the subtitles and titles were marked with Areas of Interest (AOIs) in Tobii Studio and automatically created clusters were used to identify "areas with high concentrations of gaze data points".[20]

4 Results

The hypotheses on visual attention were tested by analysing the eye movements of the 45 participants to determine whether integrated titles affect the reading

---

[19] Chandler & Sweller define "split attention" as the result of the divided attention of a learner due to "multiple sources of information" (1991: 295), which can be – in the context of film material – transferred to splitting attention between image and title (and sound) as sources of information. More attention towards the image – rather than on the subtitle or title – was considered a positive effect as easier and faster information processing is more likely (cf. Drescher 1997: 151; Grady 1993).

[20] For further information, see Tobii Studio user manual, pages 67ff (clusters) and 76ff (AOIs): http://www.tobii.com/Global/Analysis/Downloads/User_Manuals_and_Guides/ Tobii_UserManual_TobiiStudio3.2_301112_ENG_WEB.pdf [2015-10-09].

time, the split attention on image and title area and the gaze behaviour compared to the English native speakers. Another focus was the impact of the individual placement on reaction time respectively time to first fixation. In the following summary of the results, "OV" is used to describe the original version the English-speaking participants watched. The traditionally subtitled version is abbreviated to "TS" (traditional subtitles) and the version with integrated titles to "IT" (integrated titles).

4.1 Eye tracking results

Based on the study in Fox (2012), it was assumed that by individually adjusting the formatting of a title, its font and placement, the reading time per title would decrease compared to the traditional counterparts. The adjustments allow for faster processing (e.g. by creating a stronger contrast) and the placement, which is closer to the focal points, motivates the audience to return to exploring the image faster. The reading times of the participants were calculated by measuring the durations of the fixations and saccades in the area of the title – expressed as total visit duration (TVD). The reading time for every subtitle by each of the 15 German participants in the second group (in the following referred to as "TS participants") and for every title by each of the 16 German participants in the third group (the "IT participants") was recorded. As the Shapiro-Wilk test showed a deviation from a normal distribution, the two data sets – the reading times of the TS participants and the IT participants – were compared using the Wilcoxon test: W = 1675877, p < 0.001.[21] The following descriptive mean (m) and standard deviation (sd) values indicate the differences between total visit duration:

$$(1) \quad \begin{aligned} &\text{m(TVD\_TS)=1.835s} \quad \text{sd(TVD\_TS)= 1.159s} \\ &\text{m(TVD\_IT) =1.570s} \quad \text{sd(TVD\_IT) =1.069s} \end{aligned}$$

The difference between the two mean values is about 0.265s – a reduction of 14.4% of the reading time for integrated titles compared to traditional subtitles (see Figure 6).[22]

Another measurement of visual attention was defined as split-attention between image and title area. As the first hypothesis predicted shorter reading time, the second hypothesis predicted that the participants with integrated titles

---

[21] As the error probability p is clearly below the tolerable 5% (0.05), there is a significant difference between the two data sets.

[22] As the font in this study was rated inferior and less readable compared to *Gill Sans Bold*, the font that was ultimately chosen, the final eye tracking study on *Joining the Dots* set for 2015 might result in both shorter reading times and an improved aesthetic experience.

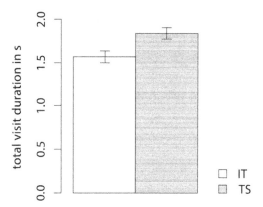

Figure 6: Comparison of the average total visit duration (s) of the IT und TS participants

spend more time exploring the image than looking at the title. To test this hypothesis, TVD of both the entire image and the (sub)title area during the stimulus, meaning the time between the (sub)title fading in and out, was measured. For all four data sets (TVD of the image TS/IT and TVD of the title area TS/IT), the Shapiro-Wilk test showed a non-normally distributed population. The Wilcoxon test then showed highly significant differences between the corresponding data sets:

(2) wilcox.test(TVD_IT_IMAGE, TVD_IT_TITLE):   W = 4400522, p < 0.001
wilcox.test(TVD_TS_IMAGE, TVD_TS_TITLE):   W = 2769346, p < 0.001
wilcox.test(TVD_TS_IMAGE, TVD_IT_IMAGE): W = 2616334, p < 0.001
wilcox.test(TVD_TS_TITLE, TVD_IT_TITLE):   W = 2217703, p < 0.001

m(TVD_TS_IMAGE) = 3.555 s   m(TVD_TS_TITLE) = 1.835 s
m(TVD_IT_IMAGE) = 3.306 s   m(TVD_IT_TITLE) = 1.570 s

The results show that on average the TS participants focused on the subtitle area for 51.6% of the title display duration, on average 1.83s of 3.55s. For integrated titles, the participants focused on the title area for around 47.5% of the time (on average 1.57s of 3.3s.; see Figure 7).

Due to the very short time frame in which the (sub)titles are visible, the difference seems quite small. Therefore, the explorative behaviour right before and after the stimulus should be examined. For the time frame right before the (sub)title is blended in, a look at the reaction times might be insightful. A reaction time of 0 means that a participant had already focused on the area before the (sub)title was shown. This value should only occur rarely, e.g. between sequential (sub)titles containing long sentences.

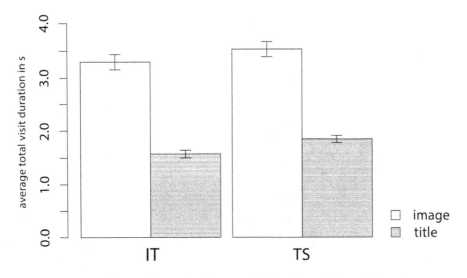

Figure 7: Comparison of split-attention in IT and TS participants

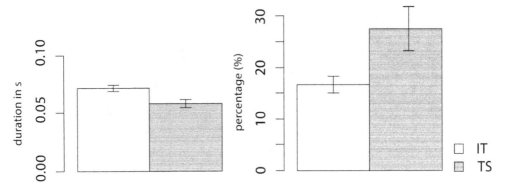

Figure 8: Mean reaction time and average percentage of 0 values of TS and IT participants

Figure 8 shows the reaction times and corresponding average number of the value 0. For the IT participants, the value 0 occurred on average 23.1 times and 33.4 times for the TS participants; this corresponds to 16.5% of all reaction times for the IT participants and about 27.5% for the TS participants. Therefore, the TS participants focused on the title area before the stimulus significantly more often while the IT participants remained focused on the image for a longer time. An analysis of how long the audience's gaze remained in the title area after the (sub)title had already faded out is planned for a follow-up study.

The third hypothesis stated that the IT participants are more likely to fixate the same focus points as the native participants. The hypothesis was tested using

Figure 9: Comparison of the automatically created clusters OV/TS/IT (*Joining the Dots*, UK 2012)

a random sample of corresponding subtitles and titles and automatically generated cluster areas. These clusters are areas with accumulated fixations and are generated by the Tobii Studio software (see Figure 9).

These clusters were created for ten random scenes[23] and considered only when they were fixated by at least half of the corresponding participant group. Four clusters weren't evaluated as they couldn't be interpreted clearly while 23 clusters were evaluated. During this sample, the most relevant focus points – the clusters which at least 50% of participants viewed – were fixated by an average

---

[23] Excluding scenes in which a subtitle (TS) was divided into several titles (IT) and scenes that consisted exclusively of a black background. The first few scenes only consisted of the film title and prologue and were therefore skipped. After that, every tenth scene was used. For detailed information, see Fox (in preparation).

87.87% of the OV participants. Clusters at the same spot or very close were fixated by an average 75.3% of the TS participants and 83.3% of the IT participants.
Thus, the integrated titles increased the mean number of participants that fixated the focus points of the English natives by 10.6%. Additionally, the sample
showed that, on average, 88.1% of the TS participants fixated the subtitles while
about 98.2% of the IT participants fixated the integrated titles – an increase of
11.5%. All in all, a higher percentage of the IT participants in this random sample
focused both on the focus points of the OV participants and the displayed titles.

   The hypothesis of increased reaction time due to integrated titles is based on
the assumption that an audience that is used to subtitles has already learned
to switch focus to the bottom area as soon as someone in the film starts speaking. For integrated titles, one can assume that the title area isn't focused until the
fade-in effect initiates the eye movement (cf. "involuntary attention", Prinzmetal,
McCool & Park 2005: 74). To test this hypothesis, areas of interest were defined
for every subtitle and title. They allow measurements of the reaction time, meaning the duration between when the (sub)title fades in and the first fixation in the
corresponding area of interest ("time to first fixation", TFF). The data of the 15
TS and the 16 IT participants were compared and, as the Shapiro-Wilk test was
significant for both data sets, the Wilcoxon test was applied: W = 2281026, p <
0.001. The reaction time of the IT participants (0.074s) was – taking the 0 values into account – on average 28.9% higher (0.017s) than for the TS participants
(0.057s). Omitting the 0 values, the increase was about 25.9% – from 0.069s for
TS participants to 0.087s for the IT participants; see Figure 10).

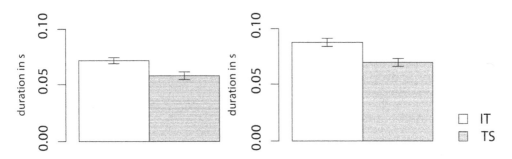

Figure 10: Mean reaction time with (left) and without (right) the 0 values

4.2 Questionnaire results

In addition to recording the eye movements and analysing the attention and reaction of the participants, a questionnaire on the aesthetic experience was also

part of the study. As eye movements cannot tell us very much about the subjective feelings of a participant, all participants with integrated titles were asked to rank several statements after watching *Joining the Dots*.[24] The questionnaire was divided into a general part with statements on information intake and a second part focusing on the aesthetic experience. The participants could rank the statements on a four-point Likert scale from 1 ("I fully agree") to 4 ("I completely disagree"). For a clearer presentation of the results, the first and second ranks were interpreted as "agreement" and the third and fourth rank as "disagreement". All 16 participants with integrated titles rated all the statements anonymously. The following statements[25] were to be ranked:

- I could easily read all integrated titles.

- I received all necessary information through the integrated titles.

- I would prefer integrated titles to traditional subtitles.

- I could spend more time exploring the image compared to traditional titles.

- Due to the integrated titles, I was aware of more details in the image.

- The integrated titles didn't cover important elements in the image.

- The integrated titles distracted me less from the image compared to traditional subtitles.

Figure 11 shows that more than half of the participants agreed or fully agreed with the statements. While still scoring more than 80% agreement, statement 5 on improved detail perception was agreed with least. In addition to the statements, the participants were asked to rate their aesthetic experience ("How would you rank your overall aesthetic experience with the integrated titles?"). Nine out of the 16 participants ranked it 1 ("very good"), 7 rated it 2 ("good"). None of the participants ranked it 3 ("satisfactory") or 4 ("unsatisfactory").

---

[24] The questionnaire was designed following the recommendations on http://www.wpgs.de/content/blogcategory/87/355/ [06.01.2015].

[25] It cannot be ruled out that a less positive wording of the statements would influence the overall agreement.

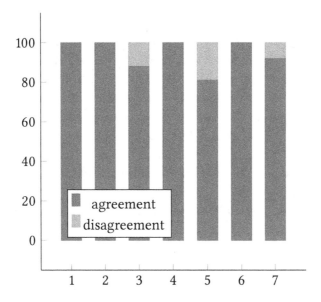

Figure 11: Distribution of agreement and disagreement with the statements

5 Discussion

This paper investigated whether integrated titles represent an advantageous alternative to traditional subtitles. The study used both eye tracking and questionnaire data to determine whether integrated titles offer improvements over traditional subtitles concerning visual attention, information absorption and aesthetic experience. In the first step, 14 native English-speaking participants watched the original version of the short documentary *Joining the Dots*. This allowed a determination of the audience's undistracted focus and yielded gaze data that could later be compared to the gaze data from participants reading (sub)titles. The analysis of the recorded focus points served as orientation for the best possible placement of the integrated titles. In the second step of the study, traditional German subtitles were added to the documentary and shown to 15 German speakers with little or no knowledge of English. This data could later be compared to the gaze behaviour of the third group, 16 native-speakers of German with little or no knowledge of English watching the documentary with integrated titles.

The average reading time for integrated titles decreased by about 14.4% compared to the average reading time for traditional subtitles. While (sub)titles where visible, IT participants focused on the title area on average 47.5% of the time and TS participants 51.6%. This indicates that integrated titles motivate the audience to return to the actual focal point in the image faster and spend more time exploring the image while the title is visible. This is also supported by the low number of participants that fixated the title area before the title was faded in: Only about 16.5% of all recorded reaction times of the IT participants was 0 (therefore they focused on the area before the recording time and display of the title; compare to "astray fixations" in Rajendran et al. 2013). For the TS participants, the percentage of reaction times amounting to 0 was 28.7%. Therefore, about 1 out of 4 TS viewers wasted time they could have spent on the image by fixating the subtitle area too early (excluding successive subtitles that are part of the same sentence). A possible interpretation is that integrated titles trigger a more efficient reading, as both reading time and wasted time are reduced.

Looking at a random sample of ten (sub)titles and the therein defined 23 important areas of attention, the gaze behaviour of the TS and IT participants was compared to that of the 14 English native speakers. The automatically generated clusters, the areas of accumulated fixations created by Tobii Studio, were defined as relevant focus points if more than 50% of the participants fixated them at least once. While on average 87.87% of the OV participants fixated the 23 focus points, 75.3% of the TS participants and 83.3% of the IT participants fixated similar areas. In addition, an increase of 11.5% of the participants that fixated the (sub)titles could be observed for the integrated titles: While on average 88.1% of the subtitles were fixated by the TS participants, this number increased to 98.2% for the integrated titles. This indicates that integrated titles allow for a more undistracted gaze behaviour and at the same time seem to motivate the viewer to fixate a higher percentage of the titles. It also invalidates the possible point of criticism that viewers might be more likely to miss a title due to the changing position.

The reaction time of the IT participants, however, increased visibly: Including the 0 values, the reaction time for integrated titles increased by 28.9%, amounting to approximately 0.057s. Excluding the 0 values, the increase was about 25.9% or 0.074s. An increased reaction time, however, cannot strictly be interpreted as a negative effect: While a shorter reaction time might be associated with less cognitive load for the viewer, a longer reaction time might also be synonymous with longer image exploration. Furthermore, the shorter reading time with a decrease of 0.265s on average seems to compensate the increased reaction time more than enough.

All in all, the evaluation of the eye tracking data shows that integrated titles can decrease the reading time and motivate the viewer to faster return to the relevant focus points. It seems less likely that the title area would be fixated before the title actually fades in and a random sample of ten scenes indicated that the focus of an audience using integrated titles is more likely to archive a similar gaze behaviour compared to the native participants. The reaction time increased.

The evaluation of the questionnaires resulted in an overall positive rating of their aesthetic experience by the German participants – especially when the integrated titles were compared to traditional subtitles. This positive feedback supports the hypothesis that differences in design and placement of (sub)titles are perceived by the audience and considerate placement can have positive impacts on the reception and information gain. Many participants that normally prefer dubbing, however, didn't seem to see a possible alternative in the integrated titles. Participants used to traditional subtitles on the other side rated integrated titles as an improvement and a feasible alternative they would like to use in the future.

Practical implications arise for all areas of film translation. Film producers should be aware of the effects traditional subtitles can have on the film's perception – especially in the light of top-grossing and award-winning Hollywood films making more profit in their translated versions than at home (Romero-Fresco 2013: 202). On the one hand, these rather basic eye tracking data already show the possible positive effect integrated titles can have on the information intake and aesthetic experience of the audience. On the other hand, a first set of basic modular guidelines for the creation of integrated titles were introduced in Fox (2015). These offer new possibilities for filmmakers to have their work translated with more respect and to create a more aesthetic experience for the target audience.

As the integrated titles for *Joining the Dots* were finalised after the third participant group watched the documentary using the eye tracker, a fourth study with 15 more German participants is planned to evaluate the possible impact of the adjusted text design and added effects. Additionally, the existing data set will be analysed with regard to the gaze behaviour directly after the title fades out. This will indicate whether the audience of integrated titles returns to the focal points in the image faster. The continuing work on integrated titles will include further development of the modular guidelines and the creation of comprehensible examples of placement and use of effects in various shot compositions without a graphic design or filmmaking background. The consideration and preservation of the typographic identity of film, e.g. the typefaces, colour sets and effects already used on text elements in the original version, is seen as a second relevant topic in the analysis of the graphical effects due to translation.[26] Additionally, further

---

[26] Presented in the talk "Reception, Information Flow and Aesthetics: Integrated Titles and Other Possible Improvements" during the *International Conference on Eyetracking and Applied Linguistics 2014* in Warsaw and *Languages & The Media 2014* in Berlin.

studies might test the possibilities of integrated titles and accessibility-related adaptions – e.g. additional colour schemes for easier speaker identifications and the visualization of sound and noises. Such elements are already used in various contexts and can also be used to indicate the way someone speaks, their volume and intonation.

Overall, the study showed that integrated titles do have the potential to improve the viewing experience and offer film producers new angles of incorporating translation into their image compositions.

Acknowledgements

For their inexhaustible support and supervision, I would like to thank Prof. Dr. Silvia Hansen-Schirra, Dr. Pablo Romero-Fresco and the MFG foundation in particular. Furthermore, special thanks go to Maik Fox, Silke Gutermuth, Rebecca Klinkig, Jan Krämer, Dimitar Molerov, Jean Nitzke, Katharina Oster and Sascha Wolfer for listening, discussing, reading and commenting on both small and larger scales.

References

Archer, Ben. 2007. Typotheque: Eric Gill got it wrong; a re-evaluation of Gill Sans. https://www.typotheque.com/articles/re-evaluation_of_gill_sans/.

Bayram, Servet & Duygu Mutlu Bayraktar. 2012. Using eye tracking to study on attention and recall in multimedia learning environments: The effects of design in learning. *World Journal on Educational Technology* 4(2). 81–98.

Brown, Andy, Rhia Jones, Mike Crabb, James Sandford, Matthew Brooks, Mike Armstrong & Caroline Jay. 2015. Dynamic subtitles: The user experience. In *Proceedings of the ACM International Conference on Interactive Experiences for TV and Online Video*, 103–112. ACM.

Caffrey, Colm. 2009. *Relevant abuse? Investigating the effects of an abusive subtitling procedure on the perception of TV anime using eye tracker and questionnaire.* Dublin City University PhD thesis.

Cintas, Jorge Diaz & Pablo Muñoz Sánchez. 2006. Fansubs: Audiovisual translation in an amateur environment. *The Journal of Specialised Translation* 6(1). 37–52.

Drescher, Karl Heinz. 1997. *Erinnern und Verstehen von Massenmedien: Empirische Untersuchungen zur Text-Bild-Schere.* Vol. 43. University of Vienna: Vienna Facultas.

d'Ydewalle, Géry & Wim De Bruycker. 2007. Eye movements of children and adults while reading television subtitles. *European Psychologist* 12(3). 196–205.

d'Ydewalle, Géry, Johan Van Rensbergen & Joris Pollet. 1985. Reading a message when the same message is auditorily available in another language: The case of subtitling. *Psychological Reports of Leuven University* 54.

Flothow, Sebastian. 2009. Eye tracking. Ein Überblick über Geschichte, Methoden und Anwendung. http://www.cs.hs-rm.de/~linn/fachsem0809/eyetracking/Eye_Tracking.pdf, accessed 2012-06-26.

Fox, Wendy. 2012. *Integrierte Bildtitel – eine Alternative zur traditionellen Untertitelung. Am Beispiel der BBC-Serie Being Human.* Johannes Gutenberg University Mainz/Germersheim Master's thesis.

Fox, Wendy. 2015. Integriti – Integrierte Titel. Ausführlicher Abschlussbericht für das Karl-Steinbuch-Stipendium 2013&2014. http://stiftung.mfg.de/de/talentforderung/projekte/integriti-integrierte-untertitel-2013-1.22151.

Grady, Denise. 1993. The vision thing: Mainly in the brain. *Discover* 14(6). 56–66.

Ivarsson, Jan & Mary Carroll. 1998. *Subtitling.* Simrishamn, Sweden: TransEdit.

Joos, Markus, Jens R. Helmert & Sebastian Pannasch. 2005. Blickbewegungsmessung und praktische Anwendungen. TS Dresden. http://tu-dresden.de/die_tu_dresden/fakultaeten/fakultaet_mathematik_und_naturwissenschaften/fachrichtung_psychologie/i3/applied-cognition/publikationen/pdf/joos2005b.pdf.

Joos, Markus, Matthias Rötting & Boris M. Velichkovsky. 2002. Bewegungen des menschlichen Auges: Fakten, Methoden und innovative Anwendungen. https://tu-dresden.de/die_tu_dresden/fakultaeten/fakultaet_mathematik_und_naturwissenschaften/fachrichtung_psychologie/i3/applied-cognition/publikationen/pdf/joos2002.pdf, accessed 2012-05-23.

Just, Marcel A. & Patricia A. Carpenter. 1980. A theory of reading: From eye fixations to comprehension. *Psychological Review* 87(4). 329–354.

Karamitroglou, Fotios. 1998. A proposed set of subtitling standards in Europe. *Translation Journal* 2(2). 1–15.

Koolstra, Cees M., Tom H. A. van der Voort & Géry d'Ydewalle. 1999. Lengthening the presentation time of subtitles on television: Effects on children's reading time and recognition. *Communications* 24(4). 407–422.

Kowler, Eileen. 2006. Attention and eye movements. In Richard Krauzlis (ed.), *New encyclopaedia of neuroscience*, 605–616. Amsterdam: Elsevier.

Kruger, Jan-Louis, Esté Hefer & Gordon Matthew. 2013. Measuring the impact of subtitles on cognitive load: Eye tracking and dynamic audiovisual texts. In

Proceedings of the 2013 Conference on Eye Tracking South Africa. ACM. Cape Town.

Lambourne, Andrew. 2012. Climbing the production chain. Paper presented at 2012 Languages and The Media Conference (Berlin, 21–23 November 2012).

Lykke Jakobsen, Arnt & Kristian Tangsgaard Hvelplund Jensen. 2008. Eye movement behaviour across four different types of reading task. *Copenhagen Studies in Language* 36(1). Susanne Göpferich, Arnt Lykke Jakobsen & Inger M Mees (eds.). 103–124.

McClarty, Rebecca. 2012. Towards a multidisciplinary approach in creative subtitling. *MonTI. Monografías de Traducción e Interpretación* 4(1). 133–153.

McClarty, Rebecca. 2013a. *Film and translation: The art of subtitling.* Unpublished PhD thesis.

McClarty, Rebecca. 2013b. In support of creative subtitling: Contemporary context and theoretical framework. *Perspectives* 22(4). 592–606.

Mercado, Gustavo. 2010. *The filmmaker's eye.* New York City/London: Focal Press.

Molerov, Dimitar. 2012. *Schriftlicher Text im Film und seine Übersetzung: Die Inserts der BBC-Serie Sherlock (2010-12); aus der Perspektive von Untertiteltheorie, Comictheorie und Translationspraxis.* Mainz, Germany: Johannes Gutenberg-Universität Mainz MA thesis.

Moran, Siobhan. 2008. The effect of linguistic variation on subtitle reception. Audiovisual Translation: Multidisciplinary Approaches Conference. Montpellier, France.

Orrego-Carmona, David. 2014. Where is the audience? Testing the audience reception of non-professional subtitling. In Esther Torres-Simon & David Orrego-Carmona (eds.), *Where is the audience? Testing the audience reception of non-professional subtitling,* 77–92. Tarragona: Intercultural Studies Group.

Perego, Elisa & Fabio Del Missier. 2008. Is a reading situation better than another for subtitled film viewers. Audiovisual Translation: Multidisciplinary Approaches Conference, 19-21 June 2008, Montpellier, France.

Prinzmetal, William, Christin McCool & Samuel Park. 2005. Attention: Reaction time and accuracy reveal different mechanisms. *Journal of Experimental Psychology: General* 134(1). 73–92.

Rajendran, Dhevi J., Andrew T. Duchowski, Pilar Orero, Juan Martínez & Pablo Romero-Fresco. 2013. Effects of text chunking on subtitling: A quantitative and qualitative examination. *Perspectives* 21(1). 5–21.

Rayner, Keith. 1998. Eye movements in reading and information processing: 20 years of research. *Psychological Bulletin* 124(3). 372–422.

Romero-Fresco, Pablo. 2013. Accessible filmmaking: Joining the dots between audiovisual translation, accessibility and filmmaking. *The Journal of Specialised Translation* 20. 201–223.

Chapter 3

Crazy Japanese subtitles? Shedding light on the impact of impact captions with a focus on research methodology

Minako O'Hagan

University of Auckland

Ryoko Sasamoto

Dublin City University

This paper addresses intralingual captions called "impact captions" (Park 2009) that have become an integral part of entertainment TV programmes in parts of Asia. These captions are different from the mainstream intralingual captions designed for accessibility for deaf and hard-of-hearing viewers. Aimed at enhancing the entertainment value of a programme for hearing viewers, impact captions are designed to draw the viewer's attention to particular elements according to the TV producer's perspective. Despite the prevalent and increasing use of such captions, however, they are created without formal guidelines at the discretion of TV producers. Focusing on these novel captions which fall outside the norms of TV captions elsewhere, this paper discusses their impact on viewers while exploring methodological issues in eye-tracking research. The initial experiment results show few fixations in the caption area; despite the participants declaring that they read the captions, viewers fixate far more on the middle region of the screen where faces are shown. The paper discusses the limitations and advantages of reception studies based on eye-tracking while contributing towards further refinement of empirically-oriented reception studies in audiovisual translation (AVT) research.

1 Introduction

1.1 Aim of the paper

Over the last decade audiovisual translation (AVT) has flourished in Translation Studies, reflecting the needs of the age of multimedia and ongoing globalization

Minako O'Hagan & Ryoko Sasamoto. 2016. Crazy Japanese subtitles? Shedding light on the impact of impact captions with a focus on research methodology. In Silvia Hansen-Schirra & Sambor Grucza (eds.), *Eyetracking and Applied Linguistics*, 31–58. Berlin: Language Science Press. DOI:10.17169/langsci.b108.234

in digital communications environments. In particular, subtitling became a popular mechanism to globalise AV content relatively cheaply and quickly (Díaz Cintas 2013: 274). It also further diversified, challenging the well-established subtitling norms, as in the case of fansubbing which refers to subtitling performed by fans. Subtitles used for AV content today can therefore not only be classified according to the temporal factors of their production (real-time or pre-prepared) and linguistic dimensions (interlingual versus intralingual), but also in terms of conformity to AVT norms. Furthermore, breaking the subtitle norms applies not only to unofficial fansubs, but also to official examples of "authorial titles" (Pérez-González 2012) or "integrated titles" (Fox 2013) where subtitles are designed as part of the diegetic element of drama content on TV (e.g. BBC's Sherlock series 2010-) as well as some movies (e.g. *Night Watch* Dozor 2004). Positioned along these developments are official yet norm-breaking TV captions which have become prevalent in some Asian regions over the last two decades.

The present paper sets out to investigate the impact on the viewers of pre-prepared intralingual TV captions with novel characteristics vis-a-vis AVT norms. The intralingual TV captions in question, commonly known as "telop" in Japan, are currently used almost exclusively in parts of Asia and have been little known elsewhere. Unlike the well-established intralingual subtitles for the deaf and the hard-of-hearing (known as SDH[1]), they are designed to enhance the entertainment value of a programme primarily for hearing audiences by stressing a particular selective message from the producer's perspective. The captions which are related to speakers' utterances are usually displayed in conspicuous fonts and colours in the lower part of the screen[2]. The use of different colours in impact captions may seem comparable to colour-coding in SDH whereby providing speaker identification when there are two or more speakers in a given scene, yet is completely different in intention. For example, multiple colours even within a single caption, as shown in Figure 1, highlight the primary objective of seeking attention. In an attempt to shed light on the impact of such captions on Japanese TV viewers' reception of presented content, this study locates itself among empirically-based reception studies in AVT and attempts to fill the gap in these lines of inquiry, as highlighted by AVT scholars (e.g. Gambier 2013). Furthermore, we seek to contribute towards methodological considerations for eye-tracking research on subtitles as this area has to date remained "a largely

---

[1] In American usage subtitles are called captions and SDH is referred to as "closed captions" (CC).

[2] These captions may also be accompanied by additional effects such as sound effects and animations, constituting a multi-layered semiotic unit, but these aspects are beyond the scope of this paper.

uncharted territory with many research avenues still to be explored" (Kruger, Aszarkowska & Krejtz 2015: n.p.). For the purpose of this paper we use the terminology "impact captioning" and "impact captions" introduced by Park (2009) interchangeably with the local Japanese term "telop". As a superordinate concept the former better captures the primary function of such captions in that they are deliberately designed to impact on the viewers' interpretation (Shiota 2003).

1.2 Japanese impact captions – telop

The impact captions under study initially derived from an intention to aid viewers' comprehension, which is not dissimilar to SDH, but over time they have evolved into a blatant media enhancement tool (Kato 2012: 48–50). In the case of Japanese television the functionality of these captions is divided into roles that are: (1) informational; (2) repetitive and (3) interpretive (Shiota 2003: 72). Kimura et al. (2000) further divide the third category into: (i) explanatory text added where there is no audible dialogue and (ii) elicitation of unspoken psychological state. It is the "interpretive" characteristics which we focus on this paper as they set these captions apart from SDH and from most official interlingual subtitles used to facilitate foreign AV content. Referring to examples in Korea where such TV captions are also extremely popular, Park (2009) highlights their "regimenting" function in relation to viewer interpretation, which he claims to be afforded by "impact captioning".

These captions reportedly originated in Japan where they are locally known as "telop" named after the image projecting equipment called Television Opaque Projector that was prevalent in the pre-computerisation era (Sakamoto 1999). As background to the various AVT forms in Japan, the terms subtitles (字幕), captions (キャプション) and telop are often used indiscriminately in the context of television, and general viewers are typically unaware of the technical difference between open and closed subtitles (captions) (O'Hagan 2010: 73–74). Telop are open captions which cannot be turned on and off by the viewers and may sometimes obscure SDH. As a rule of thumb TV captions used for news programmes in Japan tended to be limited to two lines, each of 12 characters. However, today the number of characters has increased even beyond 15 characters per line partly due to improving legibility of even small letters shown on TV screen (Kato 2012: 47–48). The use of telop became widespread in Japan particularly since the late 1990s, most frequently appearing in what are commonly known as variety shows (Shitara 2012) which incorporate a mixture of light entertainment content such as talk shows and game shows. Added during the post-production process, telop texts are usually displayed using disproportionately large fonts in multiple

Figure 1: A typical variety show scene with telop (Honmadekka broadcast 13 July 2013, Fuji TV)

colours, occupying a sizable portion of the screen (see Figure 1 for an example). While top corners of the screen are often used for referential titles to give a quick identification of the programme and/or the programme segment in smaller fonts the captions on which we focus in this paper are mainly displayed horizontally at the lower part of the screen in noticeably larger fonts.

The conspicuous nature of impact captions in terms of their visual appearance and the fact that they are open captions imply that TV viewers have by now become accustomed to them as an integral part of TV programmes and of TV viewing experience. In fact, earlier studies (e.g. Sakamoto 1999; Kimura et al. 2000) had already signalled a concern over the way in which some TV viewers admit that they could not derive the maximum enjoyment of the programme without these captions. While SDH facilitated social integration of hearing impaired viewers (Díaz Cintas 2013: 279) with the neutrality of such captions being of paramount importance, impact captions display a distinct characteristic of viewer manipulation (Shiota 2003; O'Hagan 2010; Sasamoto 2014). In this sense impact captioning is more akin to advertising with a highly biased intention than being an impartial comprehension aid. Japanese impact captions reflect the perspective of the TV producers who determine their wording and positions. The fact that they are generated without any formal guidelines other than a general compliance with aspects of the TV broadcasting code (Private Communication, Mori 2014) raises a concern over potential overuse, misuse and abuse of such captions as occasionally reported by viewers to the Japanese Broadcasting Ethics and Program Improvement Organization (BPO). For example, a case of bogus captions broadcast in August 2011 on a Tokai TV programme concerned the wording used in captions for sacks of rice offered as a prize, clearly implicating them for radiation contamination. This touched the raw nerves of the rice producers as well as the viewers at the time of the Fukushima nuclear power plant crisis, following the devastating earthquake and tsunami in Japan. It was later revealed that the captions in question were created by a contracted caption-maker as a joke, not intended to go to air, but, were inadvertently broadcast without intervention. This was considered a serious oversight and led to the axing of the given programme (Kato 2012: 36–37). Behind such an incident was not only the issue of quality control procedures, but also the relative ease in generating and inserting such captions due to computerisation, which clearly contributed (Kato 2012). Above all, this case illustrated the potential influence that such captions can exert on viewers. Despite the potentially serious consequences that impact captions could cause as demonstrated in the above incident, they have now become part of the entertainment television programme format in Japan without any serious public debate on their increased use. They are distinct from other types of official captions used on TV elsewhere, given their highly biased and also often extremely playful nature. Such characteristics point to the importance of understanding their impact on viewers.

1.3 Focus on viewers of impact captions in the literature

The fact that the application of these captions is currently limited to parts of Asia is reflected in the lack of reported research as far as English language publications are concerned with a few exceptions; Park (2009) discusses impact captions in Korea while O'Hagan (2010), Sasamoto (2014) and Maree (2015) focus on telop in Japan. These authors highlight potential impact on the viewers of the prevalent use of such captions on television without empirical data on the actual viewers. Commenting on AVT research directions to date, Gambier (2013: 57) calls for "more experimental studies on the viewer's processing habits, reading strategies and reception patterns" True to this observation the same absence seems to be applicable to research on impact captions. The present paper therefore seeks to address the gap in empirically-based reception studies.

To date studies on impact captions have generally focused on analysing the design of the captions drawing on theoretical explanations. For example, Shiota (2001, 2003 and 2005) and Sasamoto (2014) discussed an interpretive role of impact captions on the basis of relevance theoretic framework (cf. Sperber & Wilson 1986), highlighting cognitive and affective mutuality raised between the viewers and the captioned speakers on TV via the TV producers' lens. In turn Maree (2014) analysed impact captions used for the utterances of transgender personalities who are frequent guests in variety shows on Japanese TV from a sexuality and gender studies perspective. Maree argues that these captions can be seen as a manifestation of hidden desire as well as a public stance by the TV station and by society at large on the sexuality of individuals from these minority groups. In turn, Shitara (2012) used a corpus of impact captions from NHK variety shows to highlight the diachronic changes in frequency of the use of such captions and their contexts of use from the 1960s to the 2000s. She demonstrated the dramatic increase in use of these captions and also qualitative changes in their function, highlighting their use to "hook" the viewers and to add a "live-show feel" to the recorded programmes. However, reception studies have been scarce and among the few in this category is an earlier study by Kimura et al. (2000) who surveyed university students to gauge viewer perception of impact captions. It revealed evidence of habitualisation of seeing such captions with the majority of respondents (92.3% of 183 valid responses) highly conscious of the use of telop and most of them (84.6%) considering such captions to be an integral part of the whole entertainment package. In consideration of the rapid increase in the use of impact captions in recent years (Kato 2012: 50) and the particular gap in reception research which provides more objective empirical evidence we direct our attention to the viewers. In particular we aim to explore methodological issues pertinent to reception studies and investigate the applicability of eye-tracking to a relatively unexplored type of caption so as to provide useful insights onto less-known regional practices and also the research methodology in AVT.

Following this introduction, the next section discusses research contexts with a focus on prior work on AVT reception studies based on eye-tracking. This is followed by a section devoted to research design focused on methodological issues before describing our pilot study using an eye-tracker. Findings from the pilot study are then discussed, including our reflections on methodological issues before our brief conclusions are summarised.

2 Research Landscape: AVT reception studies with eye-tracking

The lack of empirically-based reception studies in AVT can be linked to a number of factors. As is well acknowledged by AVT scholars, understanding the viewer reception of AV content is fraught with difficulties from a methodological point of view due to the many variables which are not only attributable to the multimodal nature of AV stimuli but also to viewers themselves. In this section we survey the related literature on eye-tracking studies focused on subtitles in order to position our work.

2.1 Interlingual subtitle studies using an eye-tracker

In recent years, due to advances of technology, eye-trackers have become more user-friendly and increasingly employed in AVT research (see Perego 2012) whereby providing researchers with a means to gather empirical data to help understand viewers' cognitive processing of different elements of AV content including subtitles. Earliest well-known eye-tracking studies applied to subtitles came from the field of experimental psychology such as by scholars at the Belgian School, going back to the 1980s. For example, focusing on the multimodal contexts of AV viewing, d'Ydewalle, Muylle, and van Rensbergen (1985) investigated the allocation of viewer attention to interlingual subtitles by using fixation measures. The study found that only one or two words were fixated in a subtitle, with a conclusion that not much time is spent on reading subtitles although a later study (d'Ydewalle, Van Rensbergen & Pollet 1987) found 30% of the time was spent in the subtitle area when subtitles were shown. Processing of information from multiple sources can be cognitively demanding due to multiple attention shifts, as argued on the basis of early-selection theories of attention (e.g. Treisman 1968). Early-selection theories posit that incoming stimuli are filtered at an early stage so as to avoid all stimuli from becoming subject to subsequent full semantic processing.

However, the opposing idea that reading subtitles is cognitively not particularly taxing and viewers can comprehend the AV content despite the competing stimuli has been suggested by a number of eye-tracking studies (e.g. d'Ydewalle and Van Rensbergen 1989, Grimes 1991). Similarly, d'Ydewalle & Gielen (1992: 425) had concluded that "when people watch television, the distribution of attention between different channels of information turns out to be an effortless process". Such findings are further supported in a more recent study: Perego et al.

(2010) have suggested that subtitles are a cognitively effective mechanism to be used for the consumption of foreign AV content without hindering the process-ing of other visual information. Perego et al. (2010) further showed that there is an absence of trade-off between image (scene) processing and text (subtitle) pro-cessing. Furthermore, observing the different attention pattern shown to differ-ent lengths of subtitles by adults and children, the study on TV interlingual sub-titles by d'Ydewalle & De Bruycker (2007) found that two-line subtitles induced a more regular reading pattern than one-line subtitles. The authors suggested that the former are more information-rich, possibly providing the type of information which cannot be inferred from watching the scenes, hence more fully-processed than one-line subtitles. They further suggest that individuals may adjust fixation flexibly in reconsidering the text which may have previously been already pro-cessed. These explanations point to the role of information redundancy which will affect subtitle reading patterns.

In AVT research eyetrackers have served to assess and inform effective subtitle translation strategies and formats on the basis of viewers' cognitive effort (e.g. Ghia 2012). In particular, during the last 5 years a cluster of studies appeared specifically focused on the less mainstream subtitling, addressing diversifying AVT practices which challenge established subtitle norms. For example, a study investigated cognitive strain on viewers who are faced with competing textual in-formation shown simultaneously in pop-ups together with interlingual subtitles (e.g. Caffrey 2009). This study used a DVD product of Japanese TV anime which contained English subtitles and also extra pop-up textual explanations in English on Japanese culture-specific elements of a given scene, inspired by fansubbing approaches included to provide additional cultural comments. This study used eye-tracking data, including pupillometry, to highlight a clear case of increased cognitive effort resulting in a higher percentage of skipped subtitles with less gaze time spent on subtitles when the pop-up texts were shown on screen con-currently, especially with the presence of two-line subtitles. According to the interview data in the same study the viewers were found to perceive the speed of the subtitles to be somewhat faster in the presence of the pop-up information although the speed was unchanged. Another study (Secară 2011) investigated the impact of the use in subtitles of simplified spelling (known as "txt lingo" as often used in texting on mobile phones) in certain AV content such as movies watched on mobile phones. Based on the comparison of mean fixation time, fix-ation counts and regressions, the study suggested that the use of non-standard spelling did not impede the subtitle reading in comparison with the subtitles using standard spelling. Although on a small-scale (4 participants) the above results suggested a possible advantage of using a contracted form of a word to gain extra space especially for confined screens such as mobile phones (Secară 2011). Another study focused on the additional use of "innovative" surtitles (which contained extra information on language and culture-specific elements) in addition to subtitles, and empirically tested the merit of subtitling norms for limiting the amount of text (Künzli & Ehrensberger-Dow 2011). The study investigated the participants' reception capacity using eye-tracker and retrospective questions to find that viewers can process more information than typically indicated in the subtitling norms (e.g. max of 80 characters in two-lines). However, the authors were cautious in interpreting the results, suggesting to take into account the context of use and the background of the users who may or may not be familiar with a subtitling mode. Eye-tracking is also used to shed light on the positioning of subtitles (Fox 2013) to investigate whether the optimum position may divert from the standard location at the bottom of the screen. Focusing on the increasingly visible form of fan translation of popular American TV programmes, another study investigated differences in eye movements of viewers of the media with subtitles produced by non-professional translators (fans) as compared to professionals (Orrego-Carmona 2014). While pointing out that the viewer did not generally notice translation quality differences between the two translations, the study also showed, understandably, that viewers with lower competence in the source language (i.e. English) spent more time (46%) in the subtitle area than those with higher competence (23%) in relation to the total gaze time, and both groups spent more time in the image than the subtitle area.

2.2 Intralingual subtitle studies using an eye-tracker

Highlighting the lack of reception studies in AVT, Gambier (2008: 30) had also pointed out that empirically-based reception studies are nearly all focused on SDH. Such examples include those by (Jensema et al. 2000; Jensema, Danturthi & Burch 2000) whose initial study found that "the addition of captions to a video resulted in major changes in eye movement patterns, with the viewing process becoming primarily a reading process" (Jensema et al. 2000: 275). In relation to intralingual subtitles for hearing viewers, thus not SDH, a study by d'Ydewalle et al. (1991) showed that the participants spent roughly 20% of the time reading native language subtitles even though this was not necessary for them to understand the content. Given that impact captions are intralingual and primarily convey redundant information to hearing viewers, the assumption is that the viewers would generally understand the content without relying on the captions in a normal TV viewing scenario. Yet, despite the clear case of redundancy most viewers of programmes with impact captions admit to reading such captions as we found in our pilot study as well as by prior works (e.g. Kimura et al. 2000). This seems to be in line with the results by d'Ydewalle et al. (1991) to the extent that the viewers appear as if they cannot help themselves but read captions regardless of their informational value as also suggested by Bisson et al. (2014).

From a perspective of foreign language learning, a study (Bisson et al. 2014) that compared three different viewing conditions using a foreign language film with interlingual (the native language) subtitles, a reversed condition (ie a dubbed version into the native language with unknown foreign language subtitles) and the original unknown foreign language soundtrack and intralingual subtitles (unknown foreign language subtitles) has indicated that regardless of the conditions the participants read the subtitles. Their study found that there was no significant difference in the fixation duration and the number of fixations between interlingual subtitles and reversed conditions. However, this study showed that the participants spent a longer period of time looking at the image area for the intralingual subtitle condition while also under the reversed conditions they spent less time reading the subtitles than looking at the image, which makes sense. However, it is noteworthy that under all three conditions the participants were found to read subtitles even if they were foreign to them; Bisson et al. (2014: 414) suggest that the well-established automatic reading behaviour was applicable even when the subtitles were in an unknown foreign language to the participants in the intralingual subtitle condition. The authors also propose the possibility that saliency of the subtitles attracts the participants' visual attention where "the most salient feature attracts the viewer's gaze" (414). Also in the same vein Kruger, Aszarkowska & Krejtz (2015: n.p.) suggest that the way subtitles draw viewers' attention is similar to "faces" "the centre of the screen" and "contrast and movement". Furthermore, certain habitual factors are likely to come into play, for example, in relation to the participants who may be from subtitling- or dubbing-oriented countries. It was empirically shown that those from subtitling countries tend to read subtitles quicker with shorter fixation durations in the subtitle area (d'Ydewalle & De Bruycker 2007). The fact that the majority of adult Japanese viewers are versed in subtitle reading could be assumed to prompt faster reading while the use of fonts which are colourful and larger in size could give rise to saliency, pointing to efficient processing of such captions.

More recently Kruger & Steyn (2014) proposed a "reading index for dynamic texts (RIDT)" which is a quantification of reading of a subtitle by an individual. RIDT is defined as "a product of the number of unique fixations per standard word in any given subtitle by each individual viewer and the average forward saccade length of the viewer on this subtitle per length of the standard word in the text as a whole" (Kruger & Steyn 2014: 110). These authors further applied the index in a study and showed a positive correlation between RIDT and students' performance in an academic context in which video lectures delivered in English were shown with intralingual subtitles. It is noteworthy that the study found that attention distribution across different redundant sources of information affects the processing of subtitles more than the number of words or the number of lines of the subtitles. This finding is relevant to the interest of our present study while the development of the index is promising in that it could further contribute to a better understanding of the impact of subtitle reading on individual viewers, including impact captions.

2.3 Other related eye-tracking studies

Other relevant literature was found in the field of television studies. For example, a study (Josephson & Holmes 2006) investigated the effect on viewers of the design of "on-screen enhancements" on TV by which the authors referred to concurrently displayed information using "split screen" "bulleted summary of news developments" "a continuous crawl or ticker of headlines moved across the bottom of the screen" or "corporate logos and/or story logos". The authors sought to understand if such enhancements simply "clutter the screen or add content for the viewers". Using eye-tracking the study investigated how screen design influenced the viewer's distribution of fixation by setting up three different screen arrangements as in: (1) a standard screen; (2) a screen with a crawler and (3) a screen with a headline bar and crawler. The study found that the presence of the crawler and also the headline bar both contributed to more visual attention given to the respective areas at the expense of the fixation time of the main screen area while the text headline did not take away fixation time from the crawler (Josephson & Holmes 2006: 161). The study also found that the presence of a crawler did not negatively affect the recall of the main story while the headline helped the recall of the specific headlined content but at the expense of other information aurally delivered (ibid). In arguing for a positive correlation between screen designs for the information presentation and the viewer recall of the content, the authors drew on dual-processing theories to explain television viewing experience which involves simultaneous processing of multiple information sources. The dual-processing theoretical framework supports that the viewers can retain in their working memories information concurrently presented visually and aurally, provided that they do not cause cognitive overload and they are related (Mayer & Moreno 1998).

Even though the genre of the TV programme is different from our study, the above study is relevant to our interest in understanding the effect on viewers of impact captions which can be treated as added onscreen enhancements. Similarly, an eye-tracking study (Matsukawa, Miyata & Ueda 2009) designed to test the information redundancy effect associated with the use of impact captions in Japanese news programmes has some relevance to our study. By setting up a control group who watched the same news programmes with such captions being blurred out the authors tested the impact of such captions. In this study eye movements indicated that the onset of new captions tended to attract the viewer's visual attention albeit with individual variations. Also, the time to a first fixation indicated that the viewers prioritise certain types of captions in the order of relevance to the news item (e.g. captions on the top of the screen indicating the name of the programme may be ignored). The comparisons between the stimuli with and without the captions indicated a trade-off in terms of the fixation between the caption and the image areas. Their recall test suggested that the captions assist a better recall of the content while too much focus on certain captions highlighting partial elements could impede the full processing of auditory information, in turn misleading the viewer's understanding of the full content.

Another area which we found relevant includes aspects of usability studies of websites using eye-trackers. For example, we were interested to understand how peripheral vision may be treated in eye-tracking studies. Nielsen & Pernice (2010: 6–7) explain that peripheral vision as low-resolution viewing is not captured by eye-tracker unlike foveal vision (high-resolution viewing) which is captured as a fixation. In the context of website viewing, Nielsen and Pernice state that peripheral vision "allows users to be aware of the general layout of a Web page even though they are not looking at all the elements" (9). However, the point they stress is that although eye-tracking is based on the mind-eye hypothesis to hold that fixations suggest cognitive processing, "it is not inherently good or bad for a certain [web] design element to attract fixation or be ignored" (Nielsen & Pernice 2010: 10). This seems to imply a limitation of eye-tracking studies in understanding viewers' response to impact captions as they may fall under peripheral, rather than foveal vision, thus not captured as fixations. In our study we used types of TV programmes which are of a hedonic nature whose viewing experience is likely to be less intense and not fall into "usability" contexts since the viewers are not likely to be actively looking for specific information. We found that more eye-tracker-based studies are focused on news genres than pure entertainment genre as in our case, which makes performance testing less clear-cut for us. With these issues in mind, the prior studies still provide useful pointers to our research design as discussed in some detail in the next section.

3 Research design and methodological consideration

As illustrated above, AVT research using eye-tracking is becoming more sophisticated with an increasing awareness about methodological considerations regarding the limitations as well as the advantages (e.g. Perego 2012, Kruger, Aszarkowska & Krejtz 2015). Most eye-tracking studies in AVT today tend to use mixed-methods, combining qualitative and quantitative approaches with various data collection instruments such as questionnaires, interviews and performance tests in addition to eyetracking in order to allow triangulation. In designing empirical research the question of sample size and representativeness in terms of gender, age, background, preferences etc can be critical as addressed by AVT scholars although most studies compromise in some of these aspects for practical reasons. Furthermore, in setting up a lab-based experiment ecological validity also needs to be taken into account (Jakobsen 2014).

Given the unique aspects of impact captions in comparison to other existing forms of AVT, the eye-tracking study which we report in this paper is explorative in nature with an aim to provide some useful insights into methodological considerations for similar studies in future. The present study formed part of a larger study which combined a detailed multimodal analysis of the AV stimulus which is not reported here. In the eye-tracking portion of our study we were particularly interested in understanding: (i) viewers' visual attention to impact captions; (ii) factors which potentially affect such attention; and (iii) any notable gaze pattern observable through eyetracking. Furthermore, we wished to use an authentic experiment setup, and hence experimentally tried out a portable eyeglass type eye-tracker as detailed in the next section.

In designing this study we took into consideration challenges in eliciting viewer reception of AV content in the context of AVT research. For example, Kovačič (1995) had earlier highlighted the need to distinguish viewer reception in terms of "3R's" in reference to viewer "response" such as viewer's perceptual decoding, "reaction" involving psycho-cognitive issues and "repercussion" in reference to broader issues concerning viewer attitudes and preferences. Building on this proposal, Gambier (2013: 56–57) relates viewer "response" to "legibility" of subtitles such as speed and positioning of subtitles whereas "reaction" relates to "readability" such as viewer reading rates and reading habits. The repercussion involves longer term broader impacts which will call for a longitudinal study. In relation to such divisions of viewer reception dimensions eye-tracking studies could shed some light on both viewer response and reaction by analysing the viewer's eye movements. However, we note that the nature of the captions on which we focus in our study is different from most subtitles on which eye-tracking studies were focused in AVT contexts. The impact captions provide mostly redundant information for hearing viewers albeit selected according to the TV producers' perspective and are presented in a visually conspicuous manner. Furthermore, given the high frequency of the appearance of impact captions and wide range of variables such as the length and duration as well as other added effects we were uncertain about the direct applicability of the main approaches taken by most AVT eye-tracking studies which use the fixation count and fixation duration data on the subtitles to make a claim. Given such characteristics, the literature review suggests a close correlation of our interest to an approach focused on the viewers' information processing pattern and the screen design outside the AVT field (e.g. Josephson & Holmes 2006; Matsukawa, Miyata & Ueda 2009) which could further be linked to the user response focus of some of the web design usability studies (e.g. Nielsen & Pernice 2010). As an initial study our interest was to obtain a clue as to how the viewers respond to content delivered via multiple stimuli with the conspicuous presence of impact captions which are subjectively added by the TV producer. Furthermore affective dimensions relating to the use of different colours and fonts in impact captions would be a factor in reception, yet this is something which was beyond the scope of the present study. Being fully aware of the various limitations we designed this pilot study to obtain data without control experiments while combining it with a post-task questionnaire and using a newer portable type eye-tracker.

4 Eye-tracker-based experimental study

4.1 Method

This section describes the method and approach used in our experiment. For the purpose of this experiment, we focused on the non-referential captions more related to the discourse of the speakers within a programme, which appear at the bottom of the screen.

4.1.1 The AV stimulus, participants and equipment

Our AV stimulus consisted of an extract (duration=22 minutes: 29 seconds) taken from a popular primetime Japanese TV programme by Fuji TV called *Honma Dekka [Is It Really True?]* broadcast on 13 July 2013. The length of the clip was determined on the basis of the amount of eye-tracking data required and programme segment coherence. This programme aims to provide scientific information which would be useful to viewers in some practical contexts. Furthermore such information is delivered in a comical manner with humour, compared to more formal educational programmes. There were 438 captions of various character-lengths and time-durations included in this clip. 16 Japanese native-speaker participants (female = 14, male = 2, mean age = 20.6) who are university students were recruited for the experiment. However, we needed to discard 4 participants' data, leaving the final set as n=12 (female = 10, male = 2). We set up a 32-inch TV monitor, positioned at a 2.5-metre distance from a sofa where the participant sat. This arrangement provided comfortable seating and a viewing distance within the maximum allowable space according to the specifications of the eye-tracker (Tobii Technology AB 2012). We used Tobii Glasses eye-tracker as it offered portability and met our goal to achieve ecological validity to simulate an authentic TV viewing set-up. However, a trade-off was its relatively low sampling rate at 30 Hz and also this was monocular eyetracking (i.e. the data is collected for one eye only). Furthermore we discovered the issue of head movements during the viewing session, on which we will comment later.

4.1.2 Data collection

Prior to the experiment sessions 8 IR (InfraRed) markers were attached on the frame of the TV (see one highlighted in Figure 2). These markers are used to define an Area of Analysis (AOA) which creates a two dimensional plane for the purpose of a subsequent analysis using an Area of Interest (AOI). Tobii software uses the location information defined by these IR markers in order to map the gaze data of participants on a single picture called "snapshot" of the AOA (Tobii Technology AB 2012). Following the ethical procedures stipulated by our home institution, each participant read the plain language statement about our study and signed the informed consent. They were not told about our key interest in their eye movement in relation to impact captions. The experiment was organised with one participant at a time. Following a calibration session, each participant wearing the eye-tracker settled on a sofa which was set up in a lounge style room and watched the prepared AV material. The participants were asked not to move their head once settled into a position to watch the clip. After the viewing session, each participant filled out a post-task questionnaire which was designed to collect information related to their TV viewing habits and preferences regarding telop as well as a recall test regarding the programme content.

4.1.3 Data analysis procedures

Two researchers independently watched the replay of recorded gaze overlay for all participants for an initial impression forming. These are raw gaze data collected at the 30 Hz sampling rate. Both researchers noted that the gaze plot only infrequently reached the caption areas towards the bottom of the screen, and was mostly concentrated on the middle region of the screen where people's faces were typically shown. We then looked at the heatmap for all participants to see if the fixations would match our initial impression as shown in Figure 2.

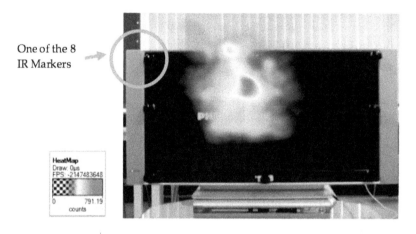

Figure 2: Heatmap of the aggregate fixation of all participants

A heatmap visualization like Figure 2 demonstrates the hot-spots where participants fixated, with the warmest colour (red) showing the most fixations, followed by yellow and then green. This initial observation and the aggregate heatmap helped us to determine areas of interest (AOI) in the subsequent eye-tracking data analysis and facilitated us to form the following post hoc hypotheses:

1. Eyes frequently fixate in the region of faces in the upper middle region of the screen

2. Visits to the bottom region where impact captions are placed are rather infrequent

Based on these initial observations we set up three AOIs as in Figure 3 for our analysis:

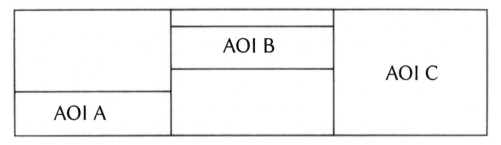

Figure 3: Setting up of three AOIs (AOI A: 1787x434, AOI B 1787x402, AOI C: 1787x1224)

We applied an approach inspired by the above-mentioned study by Josephson & Holmes (2006) who divided the screen for the purpose of analysis according to discrete regions based on the type of TV screen enhancements. Unlike other types of subtitling, impact captions have varying timing, duration and frequency as well as varying appearances as explained earlier. For this reason, we decided to follow a similar approach to Josephson & Holmes (2006) to focus on the distribution of visual attention as a percentage of fixation counts in each region, i.e. fixation counts of each region divided by those of the whole screen. Tobii's IVT Fixation Filter was applied in this study with the minimum fixation duration set at 100ms. We considered fixation values themselves have little relevance in relation to prior studies which were not focused on this type of caption. Also we compared eye-path cluster patterns of each participant to seek any specific trends.

4.2 Results

A far greater number of fixations was shown in the middle region of the screen than in the bottom caption region in terms of mean number of fixations with M=886 and M=325 respectively for the total valid results from 12 participants. However, in relation to the mean fixation duration the results showed with the middle region slightly shorter than the caption region at M=298ms and M=344ms respectively. For reference purposes the value of mean fixation for "normal reading" is reported as 200-250ms (d'Ydewalle & De Bruycker 2007). Using the ratio of fixation counts of each AOIs (e.g. Caption AOI A and Face AOI B) in relation to the total fixation counts in the whole screen (AOI C) was calculated as shown in Figure 4.

We also calculated the fixation time of the caption area (AOI A) in relation to that of the whole screen area (AOI C) with the mean ratio of all participants

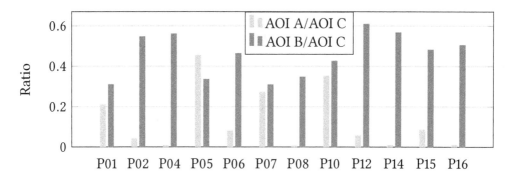

Figure 4: Fixation Count Ratio for Caption (AOI A) and Face (AOI B) Areas in relation to Total Screen Area (AOI C)

(N=12) at 12%. However, as illustrated in Figure 5, the results show a considerable variation according to each participant between 1% (P4, P8, P14) and 42% (P5) (SD=14%). For information, this compares with 20% in d'Ydewalle et al. (1991) as previously mentioned. Given the pilot nature of this study these figures may not be fully trustworthy and we did not conduct any statistical analysis. Nevertheless the results gave us a useful indication for our future study and these findings matched our initial observation of the gaze plots and fixation heatmaps, showing that considerably less visual attention was evident in the caption area (AOI A) in comparison to the face area (AOI B) in relation to the fixation on the whole screen.

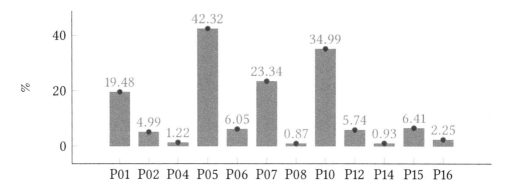

Figure 5: Ratio of Fixation Time in the Caption Area in relation to Fixation Time to the Whole Screen

The above results therefore seem to confirm our post hoc hypotheses with a far greater number of fixations (2.7 times) in the middle region of the screen where

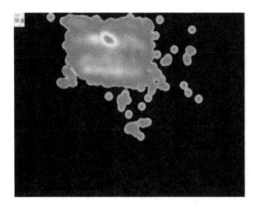 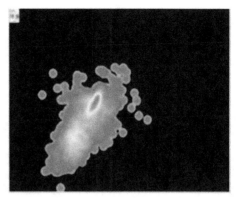

Figure 6: Heatmap for P4 (left) versus P5 (right)

mostly faces are shown.[3] While it does not help explain the viewer impact of the captions, this is in line with the known fact that faces are an eye catcher in that "[f]ace is a natural attention-grabbing visual cue" (Perego et al. 2010: 264). There are also other potential factors such as the nature of the Japanese writing system based on ideographs which may facilitate effective scanning of the key information without fixating on the caption, especially given the large font size typically used (see Figure 1). However, this is merely speculation and any further investigation was beyond the scope of this paper. In search for possible clues for some marked individual differences we next turned to particular participants. This led us to pick out the data for P5 showing the greatest fixation in the caption area and compare it with P4 who showed the least fixation time in the caption area. Figure 6 shows the respective heatmap (visualisation based on fixation count) for these two participants where it is evident that P4 tends to fixate on the upper part of the screen whereas P5 in the lower region.

Figure 7 showing cluster maps for these participants' gaze points is useful in indicating the somewhat different visual attention patterns, further confirming the upper concentration for P4 versus lower for P5.

When we cross-checked these participants' questionnaire answers for any marked differences, three questions came to our attention even though they do not directly explain the differences between them in their eye movements; P4 prefers TV programmes that do not use impact captions whereas P5 stated the opposite. However, this preference alone does not seem to justify the markedly high

---

[3] This result might indicate that there are two types of viewers in terms of fixation ratio. However, we could not find any plausible explanation for either group of viewers, in terms of both subjective (self-reported questionnaire) data and objective (eye-tracking) data.

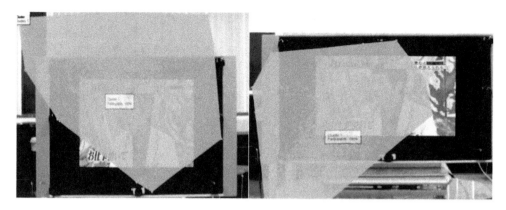

Figure 7: Cluster Maps of Gaze-Paths for P4 (left) and P5 (right)

fixations by P5 as most other participants apart from P2 and P4 also admitted they prefer captioned programmes. Regarding whether or not they would normally read impact captions if they are provided, P4 responded that she would read "all" whereas for P5 only those captions which are comments of speakers' utterance. These responses looked somewhat contradictory in relation to their preference for the use of captions in TV programmes: P4 preferred no captions but reads them all if they are there with the eye-tracking data showing few fixations on the captions. However, we did not probe the reasons for their answers. As part of the recall test which asked for the most memorable content P4 was the only respondent who gave the specific name of the chemical in tomatoes (i.e. lycopene) mentioned in the programme. When we checked the gaze plot over the relevant stretch of the programme when lycopene was discussed the gaze plot for P4 did not go to the caption area. Another difference between P4 and P5 was that while P5 would frequently engage in other activities while watching TV, P4 would rarely be engaged in other activities. Both participants chose to say "neither yes nor no" to the question on whether the captions influence their interpretation of the TV content. Incidentally, P4 was female and P5 male. In case of any gender bias we checked the only other male participant (P16) and found no specific shared characteristics between them. Although these answers suggest somewhat different TV viewing habits and preferences, there was no plausible link we could make in relation to the different gaze patterns captured in the eye-tracker. In summary, the eye-tracking data overwhelmingly showed that eyes very infrequently went to the caption area at the bottom of the screen.

5 Discussion

The eye-tracking experiment was conducted in an explorative study to consider methodological issues as well as to obtain some pointers in understanding the viewers' "reaction" and "response" to the impact captions. Relating to the reception questions, we were particularly interested in shedding light onto (i) viewers' visual attention to impact captions; (ii) factors which potentially affect such attention; and (iii) any notable observable gaze pattern. The fact that there have been no directly relevant prior eye-tracker based studies on these types of TV captions in entertainment rather than news programmes made our study more explorative.

With potential shortcomings in mind, our results still indicate that viewers generally do not fixate on impact captions, nevertheless the participants stated that they would typically read these captions. Hence, caption reading seems to take place largely outside the foveal vision with aural information likely playing the main role although it is not possible for the eye-tracking data alone to prove this. According to the eye-tracking data the participants were found to fixate far more on the middle screen region where faces were often shown. This could be explained as a natural behaviour of focusing on the image of the speaker than the captions. Although the fixation count is very low in the caption region for most participants, the mean fixation duration is somewhat longer for the captions than for the middle region of the screen with faces, possibly suggesting a somewhat greater cognitive effort for reading the captions. Based on the recall question in the post-task questionnaire most participants were able to recall key topics covered in the programme as well as the number of people who appeared on the programme. This show is particularly designed to deliver new and potentially useful information to the viewers with humour as mentioned earlier, which could prompt affective (emotional) responses from the viewers as also argued on a theoretical basis of cognitive and affective mutuality (Shiota 2003; Sasamoto 2014). In relation to the prior claim that the processing of subtitled films is cognitively effective (Perego et al. 2010), our results are inconclusive because of the relatively small amount of fixations in the main caption area even though the viewers were able to demonstrate their comprehension of the content based on some of our recall questions. Given the highly conspicuous presence of impact captions which were still mostly not fixated we could suggest that the viewers are able to divide their visual attention strategically and not necessarily be drawn to these captions while still taking them in possibly to solidify the aurally gained information. However, we will clearly need more concrete evidence to soundly prove these points.

According to the questionnaire responses none of the participants mute the sound and rely only on the captions, and all except one read all the captions, or all which relate to the speaker's utterance (which consisted of most of our captions used as our stimuli in this study). This implies that these captions are possibly never used as a primary channel for the information, yet the viewers declare they read them. This would therefore be a completely different situation from SDH although there is anecdotal evidence that the elderly population uses impact captions to compensate for their reduced hearing (it was assumed that the participants in this study all had good hearing as the demographics of the particular sample were at a relatively young age and confirmed to have normal hearing). An experiment focused on elderly viewers will therefore likely produce different results. We are aware that the way in which our study was designed was not fully conducive to identifying the effect of information redundancy by the use of captions since we did not introduce a control group, which we will need to consider in our future studies.

Upon reflecting on our method, we wondered if the choice of the particular type of eye-tracker was appropriate although it provided a relatively authentic set-up as all participants admitted that they usually watch TV on TV screens rather than on other devices such as computer screens. Although we were concerned about realism and created a living-room like setup rather than a lab situation, a few things could have been controlled. For example, a hardback chair may have been more suitable to ensure a more stationary head position than a sofa. We realized that some participants had moved their heads during the recording session despite our instructions to stay still, in some cases affecting the validity of the data which we had to remove. This pointed to the question of trade-off between control and realism, a perennial issue for any lab-based experiments, suggesting a need for more considered selection of eye-tracking tools. Furthermore, we also came to wonder about the particular design of the glass type eye-tracker sometimes proving not a good-fit for Asian facial characteristics often with a lower nose bridge than European counterparts. We note that this issue is addressed in Tobii Glasses 2. These are further points of consideration for future studies. The next question was the issue of the low sampling rate of the eye-tracker at 30 Hz. While it served the purpose of this pilot study, in future we would need to take into account the level of accuracy needed to make a certain claim by capturing more precise eye movement data. Finally, even though we considered 20 minutes to be a coherent stretch of the stimuli, in future shorter segments may be more productive with the use of control group testing by removing the captions, for example, as in the case of a study by Matsukawa, Miyata

& Ueda (2009) to be able to highlight more conclusive observations of the effect of the captions in the context of information redundancy.

6 Conclusions

We set out to apply an eye-tracker-based research methodology in order to shed light onto little discussed TV impact captions now widely used in parts of Asia while attempting to redress the lack of empirically-based reception studies in AVT. Although we were unable to arrive at a conclusive finding as to the viewer impact of the impact captions, this pilot study has given us a possible future direction to conduct control experiments whereby doctoring the captions themselves in terms of their presence versus absence. Those who are unfamiliar with these captions will likely find them invasive and even distracting because of their conspicuous nature and yet the participants in the study, who were accustomed to such captions, do not fixate on them although allegedly read them (according to their self-reporting). In this study the participants' eyes were shown to be attracted to the middle region of the screen where faces of people are typically shown despite the obtrusive nature of these impact captions. This further reminds us of the more recent approaches such as with the integrated titles used in the BBC Sherlock series where caption-like texts appear more in the middle region (see Sasamoto 2014; Dwyer 2015). However, among Japanese TV producers there seems to be tacit understanding that impact captions should not be placed too near the faces of speakers for respect especially in the case of celebrities (Private Communication, Mori 2014). Such a factor seems to be motivated by socio-cultural reasons rather than from research based on reception studies on the recipients and could form part of an interesting topic of investigation in future.

When competing information is presented in a way which is taxing on one's cognitive load as shown in the study by Caffrey (2009), there may be a trade-off in visual attention. Other studies (Perego et al. 2010: 265) suggest that it may depend on the complexity of the information and the degree of redundancy and "the individuals will not usually encounter serious difficulties in multiple-source information coming from various sources" Our study suggests the latter to be the case in distributing visual attention and dealing with multiple information sources although our stimulus mainly consisted of light entertainment which was unlikely to be taxing on one's cognitive load. However, the captions themselves presented a complex semiotic unit, combining different colours, style of font and in varying lengths sometimes accompanied by further effects. In a future study these elements will be a worthy focus in shedding further light on the impact of such additional effects on the viewers.

TV stations in Japan compete to develop a new mechanism to increase viewer ratings on their programmes and the use of impact captions is part of such a strategy to differentiate their programmes from the competition's (Private Communication, Mori 2014). Although we acknowledge the limitation of this study relating to the capacity of the eye-tracker and our method, it showed potential for these tools to be used to inform TV producers about how their captioned programmes are received physiologically by viewers and in turn potentially informing their future caption strategies.

In Translation Studies there is increasing interest in user response to translation, for example, as proposed as "user-centred translation" (Suojanen, Koskinen & Tuominen 2015) in which user experience (UX) informs translation strategies. While UX has been an area of interest in the field of human computer interaction (HCI) it is currently under explored in Translation Studies, suggesting a fruitful avenue for research (O'Hagan & Mangiron 2013: 312–318). This pilot study gave us an opportunity to further such an anchor on users and to provide clues for methodological consideration for such future studies using eye-tracking in AVT contexts.

Acknowledgement

This study was funded by the Research Support Office at Dublin City University under the 2013 Career Enhancement Award, and by the Faculty of Humanities and Social Sciences under the Performance Enhancement Scheme 2013. We would also like to acknowledge Dr. Stephen Doherty, from the University of New South Wales, for his contribution to this research project, and DCU doctoral researcher Mr. Feiyan Hu for his technical assistance with the eye-tracking tool. However, any errors and omissions are our own.

References

Bisson, Marie-Josée, Walter J. B. Van Heuven, Kathy Conklin & Richard J. Tunney. 2014. Processing of native and foreign language subtitles in films: An eye tracking study. *Applied Psycholinguistics* 35(02). 399–418.

Caffrey, Colm. 2009. *Relevant abuse? Investigating the effects of an abusive subtitling procedure on the perception of TV anime using eye tracker and questionnaire.* Dublin City University PhD thesis.

Díaz Cintas, Jorge. 2013. Subtitling: Theory, practice and research. In Carmen Millán & Francesca Bartrina (eds.), *The Routledge handbook of translation studies*, 273–287. London & New York: Routledge.

Dwyer, Tessa. 2015. From subtitles to SMS: Eye tracking, texting and sherlock. *Refractory: A journal of entertainment media* 25(1). Sean Redmond & Craig Batty (eds.).

d'Ydewalle, Géry & Wim De Bruycker. 2007. Eye movements of children and adults while reading television subtitles. *European Psychologist* 12(3). 196–205.

d'Ydewalle, Géry & Ingrid Gielen. 1992. Attention allocation with overlapping sound, image, and text. In Keith Rayner (ed.), *Eye movements and visual cognition: Scene perception and reading*, 415–427. New York: Springer.

d'Ydewalle, Géry, Johan Van Rensbergen & Joris Pollet. 1987. Reading a message when the same message is available auditorily in another language: The case of subtitling. In J. K. O'Regan & A. Lévy-Schoen (eds.), *Eye movements: From physiology to cognition*, 313–321. Amsterdam: Elsevier.

d'Ydewalle, Géry, Caroline Praet, Karl Verfaillie & Johan Van Rensbergen. 1991. Watching subtitled television: Automatic reading behavior. *Communication Research* 5(18). 540–666.

Fox, Wendy. 2013. Integrated titles as an alternative solution to traditional subtitles. In *7th EST Conference - Translation Studies: Centers and Peripheries*. Germersheim, Germany.

Gambier, Yves. 2008. Recent developments and challenges in audiovisual translation research. *Between Text and Image: Updating research in screen translation* 78. Delia Chiaro, Christine Heiss & Chiara Bucaria (eds.). 11–33.

Gambier, Yves. 2013. The position of audiovisual translation studies. In Carmen Millán & Francesca Bartrina (eds.), *The Routledge handbook of translation studies*, 45–59. London & New York: Routledge.

Ghia, Elisa. 2012. The impact of translation strategies on subtitle reading. In Elisa Perego (ed.), *Eye tracking in audiovisual translation*, 155–182. Rome, Italy: Aracne Editrice.

Jakobsen, Arnt Lykke. 2014. The development and current state of translation process research. In Elke Brems, Reine Meylaerts & Luc van Doorslaer (eds.), *The known unknowns of translation studies*, vol. 69, 65–88. Amsterdam & Philadelphia: John Benjamins Publishing Company.

Jensema, Carl J., Ramalinga Sarma Danturthi & Robert Burch. 2000. Time spent viewing captions on television programs. *American Annals of the Deaf* 145(5). 464–468.

Jensema, Carl J., Sameh El Sharkawy, Ramalinga Sarma Danturthi, Robert Burch & David Hsu. 2000. Eye movement patterns of captioned television viewers. *American Annals of the Deaf* 145(3). 275–285.

Josephson, Sheree & Michael E. Holmes. 2006. Clutter or content? How on-screen enhancements affect how TV viewers scan and what they learn. In *Proceedings of the 2006 symposium on eye tracking research & applications*, 155–162. ACM. San Diego, California.

Kato, Masao. 2012. テレビの日本語 *[Japanese language on TV]*. Tokyo: Iwanami Shinsho.

Kimura, Tamako, Akiko Hosoi, Naoko Honda, Yuri Kato, Fumiko Kawamura, Aya Koizumi, Yukoko Oosawa, Eri Suzuki & Kaori Watabe. 2000. "テレビ画面に踊る文字たちの生態学" [physiology of letters dancing on TV screen].

Kovačič, Irena. 1995. Reception of subtitles: The non-existent ideal viewer. *Translatio* 14(3–4). 376–383.

Kruger, Jan-Louis, Gnieszka Aszarkowska & Izabela Krejtz. 2015. Subtitles on the moving image: An overview of eye tracking studies. *Refractory: A Journal of Entertainment Media* 25(1). Sean Redmond & Craig Batty (eds.).

Kruger, Jan-Louis & Faans Steyn. 2014. Subtitles and eye tracking: Reading and performance. *Reading Research Quarterly* 1(49). 105–120.

Künzli, Alexander & Maureen Ehrensberger-Dow. 2011. Innovative subtitling: A reception study. In Cecilia Alvstad, Adelina Hild & Elisabet Tiselius (eds.), *Innovative subtitling: A reception study*, 187–200. Amsterdam: John Benjamins.

Maree, Claire. 2014. '変身したいです [i want to transform myself]'. ことばと社会 *[Languages and Society]* (16). 57–85.

Maree, Claire. 2015. The perils of paisley and weird manwomen: Queer crossings into primetime J-TV via telops. In Beverley Sato-Rossberg Curran & Kikuko Tanabe (eds.), *Multiple translation communities in contemporary Japan*, 124–147. New York & London: Routledge.

Matsukawa, Rei, Yosuke Miyata & Shuichi Ueda. 2009. Information redundancy effects on watching TV news: Analysis of eye tracking data and examination of contents. *Library and Information Science* 62(2). 193–205.

Mayer, Richard E. & Roxana Moreno. 1998. A split attention effect in multimedia learning: Evidence fo dual processing systems in working memory. *Journal of Educational Psychology* 90(2). 312–320.

Nielsen, Jakob & Kara Pernice. 2010. *Eyetracking web usability*. Berkeley, CA: New Riders.

O'Hagan, Minako. 2010. Japanese TV entertainment: Framing humour with open caption telop. In Delia Chiaro (ed.), *Japanese TV entertainment: Framing humour with open caption telop*, 70–88. London: Continuum.

O'Hagan, Minako & Carmen Mangiron. 2013. *Game localization: Translating for the global digital entertainment industry*. Amsterdam & Philadelphia: John Benjamins Publishing.

Orrego-Carmona, David. 2014. Where is the audience? Testing the audience reception of non-professional subtitling. In Esther Torres-Simon & David Orrego-Carmona (eds.), *Where is the audience? Testing the audience reception of non-professional subtitling*, 77–92. Tarragona: Intercultural Studies Group.

Park, Joseph Sung-Yul. 2009. Regimenting languages on Korean television: Subtitles and institutional authority. *Text & Talk-An Interdisciplinary Journal of Language, Discourse & Communication Studies* 29(5). 547–570.

Perego, Elisa. 2012. *Eye tracking in audiovisual translation*. Rome, Italy: Aracne Editrice.

Perego, Elisa, Fabio Del Missier, Marco Porta & Mauro Mosconi. 2010. Cognitive effectiveness of subtitle processing. *Media Psychology* 13(3). 243–272.

Pérez-González, Luis. 2012. Co-creational subtitling in the digital media: Transformative and authorial practices. *International Journal of Cultural Studies* 16(1). 3–21.

Sakamoto, Mamoru. 1999. 氾濫する字幕番組の功罪 [benefit and sin of overuse of subtitled programmes]. *Galac* (359). 36–39.

Sasamoto, Ryoko. 2014. Impact caption as a highlighting device: Attempts at viewer manipulation on TV. *Discourse, Context and Media* 6(6). 1–10.

Shiota, Eiko. 2003. '関連性理論とテロップの理解 [relevance theory and understanding of telop]'. *Journal of Ryukoku University* 31. 63–91.

Shitara, Kaoru. 2012. Changes in the use of telop observed with NHK variety programmes. *Mukogawa Joshidai Journal* 59.

Sperber, Dan & Deirdre Wilson. 1986. *Relevance: Communication and cognition*. Oxford: Blackwell (second edition 1995).

Suojanen, Tytti, Kaisa Koskinen & Tiina Tuominen. 2015. *User-centred translation*. London: Routeldge.

Tobii Technology AB. 2012. Tobii glasses eye tracker user manual. http://www.tobii.com/Global/Analysis/Downloads/User_Manuals_and_Guides/Tobii%20Glasses%20User%20Manual.pdf.

Treisman, Anne M. 1968. Strategies and models of visual attention. *Psychological Review* 75(84). 127–190.

Chapter 4

Subtitles vs. narration: The acquisition of information from visual-verbal and audio-verbal channels when watching a television documentary

Juha Lång

University of Eastern Finland

This paper reports the results of two experiments, in which the reception of a sub-titled television documentary was examined from the point of view of information acquisition. Experiment 1 consisted of group viewings of a short documentary narrated in Russian and subtitled in Finnish, followed by a comprehension test that included questions about the visual elements of the video and details that were mentioned in both the narration and the subtitles. Participants were Finnish natives with no knowledge of Russian, and Russian natives with good Finnish skills. In Experiment 2 the comprehension testing was paired with eye tracking methodology, and the participants were Finnish natives with no Russian language skills and Russian natives with no Finnish language skills. The results showed that the participants who could follow both the narration and the subtitles performed significantly better in the subtitle-related questions. This indicates that the availability of two overlapping information channels enhanced the acquisition of information. Experiment 2 also showed that, compared to the Russian participants, the Finnish participants performed equally well in both types of questions. In conclusion, it seems that subtitles are an effective channel for acquiring information from subtitled television programmes and they do not distract a viewer who is accustomed to them from following also the image.

1 Introduction

Reading behaviour has been one of the most researched topics in eye tracking methodology for decades (for a review of the most important findings, see Rayner 1998; 2009). The studies have concentrated on so-called normal reading, meaning (usually printed) text on paper. Subtitled television programmes differ from

Juha Lång. 2016. Subtitles vs. narration: The acquisition of information from visual-verbal and audio-verbal channels when watching a television documentary. In Silvia Hansen-Schirra & Sambor Grucza (eds.), *Eye-tracking and Applied Linguistics*, 59–82. Berlin: Language Science Press. DOI:10.17169/langsci.b108.235

this normal condition in many ways that are bound to have an effect on reading behaviour, eye movements and the allocation of attention. The most obvious difference is the presence of multiple information channels (Gottlieb 1998). In addition to the subtitles (visual verbal channel), there is the moving image (visual non-verbal channel) and, usually but not always, an audio track, which can include spoken words (auditive verbal channel) as well as background music and/or sound effects (auditive non-verbal channel). So when reading a book, for example, you can concentrate only on the text and there is only one type of information to process, namely visual verbal information. In contrast, when watching subtitled television programmes there are multiple partially overlapping information channels that battle for the viewer's attention and cognitive resources. This means that the viewer has to integrate the information from the different channels to form a consistent mental model in order to comprehend the contents of the programme. But how effective is this integration?

Studies on using subtitles in language learning (e.g. Koolstra & Beentjes 1999; Latifi, Mobalegh & Mohammadi 2011; Etemadi 2012; Ghia 2012) have shown that subtitles can be an especially effective tool in vocabulary acquisition. Mitterer & McQueen (2009) found that intra-lingual foreign subtitles (i.e. a foreign film subtitled in the language of the film) help speech perception and learning to speak the foreign language, as the foreign words are associated with the proper pronunciation. These findings suggest that some integration of the two types of verbal information happens with beneficial results.

Lee, Roskos & Ewoldsen (2013) studied how subtitles affect the comprehension of narrative film in a two-part experimental setting. In the first part, they asked a group of native English participants to write down their thoughts while watching a normal (English) or dubbed and subtitled (dubbed into French and subtitled into English) version of a film. In the second part, they asked the participants to sort the events of the film according to their similarity. The results of both experiments showed that the participants who saw the subtitled version made more remarks that referred to earlier events of the film (i.e. *back* or *bridging inferences*) while the participants who saw the normal version made more remarks that drew from the viewers' general knowledge outside the narrative of the film (i.e. *outside inferences* or *elaborations*). Bridging inferences are considered as a sign of local coherence and outside inferences are a sign of global coherence (Albrecht & O'Brien 1993, referred to in Lee, Roskos & Ewoldsen 2013). The conclusion here was that the viewer's overall comprehension of the film suffered from having to follow the subtitles and the image at the same time.

An earlier study by Lavaur & Bairstow (2011) reached similar conclusions. They had a "3 by 3" test setting, in which French natives with beginner, intermediate, or advanced English skills, 30 participants per group, saw an English film clip with no subtitles, French (interlingual) subtitles or English (intralingual) subtitles. After seeing the film extract, the participants completed a comprehension test, which included questions requiring recall of verbal information and visual information. The results showed that participants with beginner language skills recalled visual details well when no subtitles were present, but the score went down when subtitles were present. Dialogue recall score naturally went up with the subtitles. In the intermediate language skill group, both the dialogue recall and visual recall scores were largely unaffected by the different subtitling conditions. In other words, the presence or absence of subtitles did not affect the recall of visual details, and the presence of native language subtitles improved the dialogue recall scores only a little. The advanced language skill group got best scores when no subtitles were present in both recall types, and the scores were worst with the French subtitles. Lavaur & Bairstow (2011) interpreted this as a proof of the distracting effect of the subtitles, especially when they are unnecessary for comprehension as "two different types of information are transmitted through the same visual channel (images and subtitles), leading to a competition for cognitive resources" (ibid.:460). It should be noted, though, that the participants in the study Lavaur & Bairstow (2011), as well as the one by Lee, Roskos & Ewoldsen (2013), came from countries that do not use subtitling as the main method of translating foreign films, and thus they were not necessarily accustomed to watching subtitled films.

In earlier studies, d'Ydewalle and his colleagues came to different conclusions. D'Ydewalle was one of the first researchers to utilize eye tracking in psychological research on watching subtitled programmes and reading subtitles (for a review of his early studies, see d'Ydewalle & Gielen 1992). In one of these eye tracking studies, d'Ydewalle, Van Rensbergen & Pollet (1987) showed participants a German video clip with subtitles in their native tongue. The availability of soundtrack was varied: normal German soundtrack and no soundtrack. Furthermore, some of the participants had a good command of the German language, as they were advanced students of German. A surprising discovery was that the subtitles were read even when the participants understood the language of the soundtrack. This led to two hypotheses: the automaticity hypothesis and the efficiency hypothesis. The first states that reading subtitles is at least partially an automatic process. The second states that information can be acquired more quickly and more efficiently from the subtitles than from the soundtrack. This is because subtitles are read more quickly than the corresponding line is said on the soundtrack. Furthermore, as opposed to the soundtrack, which is heard only once, the subtitles can be re-read in the time frame in which they are visible.

These hypotheses have been backed up with more recent findings (d'Ydewalle et al. 1991; d'Ydewalle & De Bruycker 2007; Perego et al. 2010; Perego, Del Missier & Bottiroli 2015). D'Ydewalle et al. (1991) conducted two eye tracking experiments in which participants were shown programmes with both the soundtrack and subtitles in their native tongue: in the first experiment the participants were Americans watching an American movie with English subtitles and in the second experiment Dutch natives were shown a Dutch film with Dutch subtitles. The results corroborated the previous hypotheses as both groups spent considerable time reading the subtitles, although they had no obvious reason to do so. The first experiment also refuted the idea that reading subtitles is a learned skill, since the American participants were not used to watching subtitled movies or television programmes.

D'Ydewalle & De Bruycker (2007) examined the differences in eye movements of adults and children when reading television subtitles. In this experiment they used reversed subtitling as one variable condition, i.e. the programme's soundtrack was in the participants' native tongue but the subtitles were in a foreign language unknown to the participants. The eye tracking data showed that the differences in the reading of subtitles between children and adults are similar to the differences found in normal reading: children make longer fixations and shorter saccades. The automaticity hypothesis was further verified, since the data showed that 26% of the reversed subtitles were fixated on. Clearly, here the efficiency of subtitles as an information channel could not have been the reason for the reading behaviour, because the participants apparently did not understand the language of the subtitles and so could extract little information from them.

Perego et al. (2010) used eye tracking with word recognition and visual scene recognition tests to examine cognitive effectiveness of watching subtitled movies. In addition to normal, well-structured subtitles, they included in the stimulus some manipulated two-lined subtitles in which the segmentation of noun phrases (NPs) was syntactically incoherent, i.e. the NP was cut between its parts and the different parts of the NP were located on different lines. Based on previous research (Perego 2008) the ill-segmented NPs should have a negative effect on the processing of the subtitled material, but the results of Perego et al. (2010) did not confirm this hypothesis. The eye tracking data did not show significant differences in reading ill-segmented subtitles compared to well-segmented subtitles, apart from slightly longer mean fixation duration in the subtitle area with ill-segmented subtitles. The recognition tests showed good overall performance and there was no significant trade-off between scene recognition and subtitle recognition. This indicates that despite following the subtitles the participants were able to process the image as well, which is in contrast with the findings of Lee, Roskos & Ewoldsen (2013) and Lavaur & Bairstow (2011).

In a more recent study, Perego, Del Missier & Bottiroli (2015) compared cognitive processing of dubbed and subtitled film using various cognitive measures, including dialogue and visual scene recognition and face-name association. They found that the participants who saw the subtitled version of the film extract slightly out-performed the participants who saw the dubbed version in dialogue recognition and general comprehension of the film, while there was no significant difference in visual scene recognition.

Text seems to attract attention also in other mediums where pictorial information is presented together with text. For example, Carroll, Young & Guertin (1992) examined college students' eye movements while viewing single-caption cartoons, and found that captions were usually read before an exhaustive examination of the picture. Rayner et al. (2001) studied gaze patterns while looking at print advertisements in a test setting, where they asked the participants to imagine that they had just moved to England and were looking to buy either a new car or skin care products. They found that the task had an effect on the participants' gaze patterns. When a participant who was tasked to buy a car or skin care products saw a car or skin care advertisement, his/her eyes moved quickly to the text part of the advertisement and he/she spent considerably longer time reading the text than when looking at other types of advertisements. Images also received less attention in the advertisements that were relevant to the given task compared to other advertisements.

Later Rayner, Miller & Rotello (2008) used partly the same advertisements in an eye tracking experiment where they asked participants to either rate how much they liked the advertisements or to evaluate the advertisements' effectiveness. The results showed, in contrast to Rayner et al. (2001), that the participants used more time on the images than on the text. Furthermore, the participants' overall eye movement patterns differed greatly in the two experiments, but this was at least partly caused by differences in the advertisements that were used in the experiment. Nevertheless, Rayner, Miller & Rotello (2008) reach the conclusion that both the nature of the advertisement looked at and the observer's goals affect the eye movement patterns when looking at print advertisements. In the test setting of Rayner, Miller & Rotello (2008), the participants were probably mainly seeking factual information about the advertised products, which is more often found in the text than in the image.

It has been shown in multiple studies that when people look at movies or television the gaze is usually concentrated on the centre parts of the screen. Tosi,

Mecacci & Pasquali (1997) recorded eye movements of 10 adults while they were watching fiction and non-fiction film clips, including extracts from feature films, scientific documentaries, advertisements and news programmes. They found a strong centre-of-screen bias in the eye movement patterns and relatively little difference in the individual scan paths of the participants. Interestingly, the data also showed that textual elements, such as signs, attracted gaze, which is consistent with other findings on subtitle reading (d'Ydewalle, Van Rensbergen & Pollet 1987; d'Ydewalle et al. 1991; d'Ydewalle & Gielen 1992).

The centre-of-screen bias in gaze paths while watching television has since been verified (see, for example, Goldstein, Woods & Peli (2007); Brasel & Gips (2008)). Goldstein, Woods & Peli (2007) showed 20 participants video clips from 6 movies of various genres and recorded the participants' eye movements. Their aim was to examine, how much each participant's eye movement patterns differ, i.e. whether everyone looked at the same places on the screen, and whether there was any variation between age or gender groups. The results showed that most of the time people tend to fixate on a relatively small area, as more than half of the time the fixations fell within an area that was less than 12% of the full image area. There was some variation, though, as male participants' eye movement patterns were more uniform than those of female participants. A similar difference was found between older and younger participants: there was less variation between older participants than younger participants.

Brasel & Gips (2008) had a similar test setting. They created a 24-minute video clip, of which about a little over half consisted of content from a nature documentary and a little less than half was advertisements. They also found that the centre of the screen attracted most of the fixations, and 90% of the fixations landed inside an area which governed less than 27% of the image area, confirming previous studies by Tosi, Mecacci & Pasquali (1997) and Goldstein, Woods & Peli (2007). Despite this, a closer frame by frame analysis revealed differences in the gaze paths of participants and the difference seemed to grow slowly over time. In other words, when a scene becomes visible, people tend to make the first fixations to roughly the same places, but as the gaze begins to wander around the image area, the dispersion on the gaze paths of each individual increases. Not surprisingly, the content of the video affects this greatly: in Brasel & Gips (2008) static "network bumpers" (images of television network logos at the start of television programmes) attracted the most uniform gaze paths while in advertisements the dispersion was greater.

The present study has three aims. Firstly, it aims to shed further light on the issue of processing efficiency of subtitles. Perego et al. (2010) have proved that processing of subtitled material is effective and there is no visible trade-off between processing the image and the subtitles. Furthermore, studies of subtitles in language learning (e.g. Mitterer & McQueen 2009) have revealed the benefit of parallel processing of overlapping information channels. This leads to the hypothesis that the access of two overlapping information channels should have a beneficial effect on the acquisition of information (Hypothesis 1). Secondly, the efficiency hypothesis (d'Ydewalle, Van Rensbergen & Pollet 1987) is further tested by comparing the acquisition of information from the subtitles and the narration. The hypothesis here is that, following the efficiency hypothesis, subtitles are a more efficient channel of information than narration (Hypothesis 2). Hypothesis 2 is expected to be visible in the data as a difference in the performance in the relevant comprehension questions between the groups that used the two channels as their main channel of information. The third aim is to examine the impact of subtitles on the processing of image. Lavaur & Bairstow (2011) concluded that subtitles are a significant distraction, especially for those who do not need them for comprehension purposes, but Perego et al. (2010) found no difference between dubbing and subtitling conditions in visual scene comprehension. In the study by Lavaur & Bairstow (2011), the participants were not familiar with subtitled films, which may have affected the results. Hypothesis 3 is that subtitles do not have a negative effect on the processing of image for viewers who are accustomed to watching subtitled films or television programmes. The study approached these issues in two experiments. Experiment 1 included only comprehension testing, while in Experiment 2 it was combined with eye tracking methodology in order to get a deeper understanding of the cognitive processes while watching subtitled television documentary. This study did not concentrate on eye movements per se, but instead used the eye tracking data as a tool to visualize the participants' behaviour.

2 Experiments

The study includes two experiments: 1) group sessions with only the questionnaire; 2) solo sessions with eye tracking. Both use the same video stimulus and the same questionnaire, but the participant groups and procedure differ a little.

The video stimulus used in both of the experiments is a documentary about the Norwegian explorer and Nobel Peace Prize winner Fridtjof Nansen. The running time of the documentary is approximately 7 minutes. The only audio-verbal element of the documentary is the Russian narration and no dialogue is present. The documentary is subtitled into Finnish, and the subtitles were visible for all participant groups, i.e. the material is exactly the same for everyone. The visual elements consist mainly of black-and-white photos and short acted dramatizations that illustrate points in the story.

Russian was chosen as the language of the stimulus material for a number of reasons. Firstly, like most Finns, the Finnish participants did not understand Russian, and consequently they had to rely solely on the subtitles in order to understand the narrative. Secondly, in Russia subtitling is a little-used method of translating foreign films, dubbing being the method more frequently used. In other words, Russian people are not used to reading subtitles, which helped to shed light on Hypothesis 3.

The questionnaire included open-ended short answer questions from three categories according to the channel from which the information for the correct answer was available: image, narration, and subtitles. The questionnaire included 28 questions in total, but only 17 of them were analysed in these experiments. The reason for this is that the questions which concerned the information available only from the narration of the documentary fell out of the scope of these experiments and were thus omitted from the analysis. This meant excluding 9 of the questions. Furthermore, it was discovered in the analysis stage that one of the subtitle-related questions and one of the image-related questions proved to be somewhat ambiguous and thus difficult to analyse, so they were excluded from the analysis. This means that the analysis presented in this paper is based on 5 image-related questions and 12 subtitle-related questions.

To be more specific, the image-related questions asked about visual details that were not directly mentioned in either the narration or the subtitles. The narration-related questions asked about details that were not included in the translation, i.e. the subtitles, whereas subtitle-related questions asked about details that were mentioned in both the subtitles and the narration. For example, Nansen had a special ship designed for him for his expedition to the North Pole. The narrator mentions the name of the ship ("Fram") and the ship is shown in several photographs in the video, but the name is not mentioned in the subtitles. One image-related question asked about the number of masts that the ship had, while a narration-centred question asked the participants to recall the name of the ship. An example of a subtitle-related question would be one where participants were asked about Nansen's favourite school subjects, a detail that was mentioned in both the Russian narration and the Finnish subtitles. The questionnaire was available for the participants in Finnish in Experiment 1, and in Finnish and Russian in Experiment 2.

2.1 Experiment 1

2.1.1 Participants

The participants of Experiment 1 consisted of 14 native Finnish speakers and 20 native Russian speakers. The Finnish natives were students and staff of the University of Eastern Finland. Most of the Russian natives were students of Petrozavodsk State University, but also included some students and staff of the University of Eastern Finland. The Finnish natives had little or no skills in Russian, and the Russian natives were either studying or had studied Finnish at university level and thus were expected to have sufficient Finnish language skills to be able to understand the subtitles in the stimulus video. The mean age of the groups was 21.5 for the Finnish (SD=0.73) and 23.0 for the Russians (SD=1.24). Both groups were strongly lopsided in terms of gender distribution as there were only 4 males in the Finnish group and 3 males in the Russian group.

2.1.2 Method

The data in experiment 1 was collected in several group sessions, which were similar in overall procedure save for one exception, detailed below. The participants were first verbally instructed about the procedure of the test session. They were told in advance that their comprehension of the documentary would be tested after seeing the video. The participants saw the stimulus video in a classroom with a data projector, white screen and sound system. After watching the documentary, the participants completed the written questionnaire. An exception to this procedure was the session that was held at Petrozavodsk State University, where the participants watched the documentary in a computer lab, each on a computer monitor of their own and wearing headphones. Each session took approximately 25 minutes in total.

The questionnaires were analysed binomially in terms of correct answers and the binomial data was compared between the language groups with Pearson's χ^2-test with Yates' continuity correction (henceforth χ^2-test). Statistical analysis was done using the statistical software package R (version 3.1.0).

2.1.3 Results

Figures 1 and 2 below show the percentages of right answers to the questions concerning the image and the subtitles, respectively. For the analysis the questions were grouped according to their type and thus the numbering seen here is not the same as on the questionnaire.

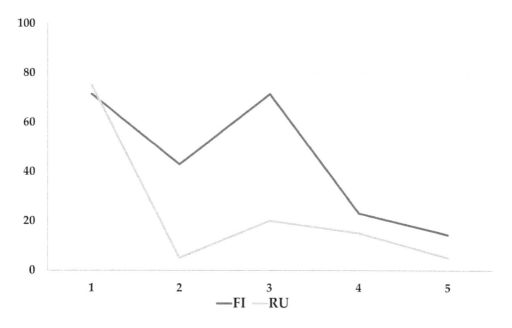

Figure 1: The percentage of correct answers in Finnish and Russian groups to the questions (1-5) concerning the image of the stimulus video.

When the image-related and subtitle-related questions were analysed as one group, the overall performances of the Russian and Finnish participants were very even and no statistical difference was visible ($\chi^2(1) = 0.010, p = 0.921$). Nevertheless, when the analysis was done separately for the two question groups, differences began to emerge. The Russian participants got slightly better scores than the Finnish participants in the subtitle-related questions (see Figure 2) and the difference is statistically significant ($\chi^2(1) = 3.90, p = 0.048$). In turn, the Finnish group performed better on the questions concerning the image of the stimulus video (see Figure 1), and here the difference is also statistically significant ($\chi^2(1) = 7.22, p = 0.007$).

2.1.4 Discussion

The results of Experiment 1 seem to support the initial hypotheses. The Russian group performed better in almost all of the subtitle-related questions, which confirms Hypothesis 1. It has been shown in previous research (d'Ydewalle, Van Rensbergen & Pollet 1987) that subtitles are usually automatically read when they are available even when they are not necessary for understanding the spoken information. This makes it reasonable to assume that also in this experiment the Russian participants followed the subtitles, which means that information was

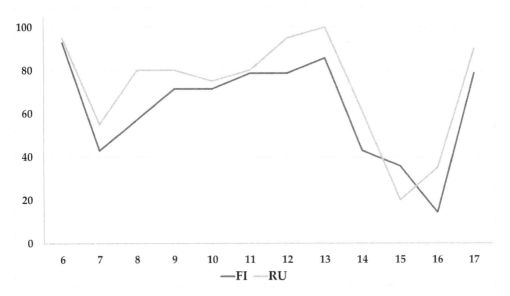

Figure 2: The percentage of correct answers in Finnish and Russian groups to the questions (6-17) concerning the subtitles of the stimulus video.

absorbed better when the same information came from two overlapping channels, namely the narration and the subtitles. In light of Paivio's dual-coding theory, which states that presenting verbal information with consistent non-verbal information improves processing and recall (Paivio 1986), the result is as expected. It should be noted, though, that here both of the information channels were verbal, even though they are in two different languages. Nevertheless, the benefit of parallel processing of visual and auditory channels was evident.

The Finnish group got a noticeably better score in the image-related questions. This result is consistent with Hypothesis 3. Subtitling is the main method of translating foreign films and other television material in Finland, and Finnish people get used to reading subtitles and watching subtitled programmes from an early age. In Russia, dubbing is the preferred method of translating audiovisual material, as is the tendency with major languages (languages with a big enough user-base to make dubbing an economically valid option). Thus Russian viewers are not accustomed to reading subtitles and they are not as effective as Finnish viewers in processing subtitled audiovisual content. This phenomenon was examined more closely in Experiment 2 with the help of eye tracking methodology.

2.2 Experiment 2

Experiment 2 was a continuation of Experiment 1. While Experiment 1 examined the difference in information acquisition between people who could follow only the subtitles and people who could follow both the narration and subtitles, here the goal was to test the difference between people who have access to only one of the information channels.

2.2.1 Participants

The participants of Experiment 2 consisted of 20 Finnish native speakers with little or no Russian skills and 20 Russian speakers. Four participants in the Russian group were omitted from the analysis because they were Russian-Finnish bilingual, and another three because they had good Finnish skills (by their own assessment). This made a total of 13 participants in the Russian group in the analysis of questionnaire data. The data of one Russian participant had to be omitted from the analysis of eye tracking data because of quality issues. The participants were mostly students and staff of the University of Eastern Finland. Again, the gender division was somewhat uneven, since there were only four males in the Russian group and eight males in the Finnish group. The mean ages of the groups were 24.1 (SD = 0.71) for the Finnish group and 31.2 (SD = 4.7) for the Russian group. As can be seen, the Finnish group was fairly homogenous with respect to age variation (age range 19-30) while in the Russian group the variation was larger (age range 17-74). This can be explained by the fact that while the Finnish participant groups only included university students, in order to get a large enough Russian participant group, the invitation to participate in the experiment was not restricted to students only and some non-students also participated.

2.2.2 Method

The biggest differences between Experiment 1 and 2 were the inclusion of eye tracking methodology and the lack of Finnish language skills in the Russian group in Experiment 2. The use of eye trackers also meant that testing had to be done in solo sessions.

The participants' eye movements were tracked with SMI Eye Tracking Glasses 2.0 (SensoMotoric Instruments GmbH, Teltow, Germany), which have a binocular sampling rate of 60 Hz. The data was recorded with SMI iViewETG (version 2.1.0) on a Windows 7 laptop connected to the eye tracking glasses. The video stimulus was shown on a separate computer, an Ubuntu distribution of Linux operating system with a 21-inch LCD display and over-ear headphones to minimize the possibility of distractions. The participant sat on a comfortable office chair, about 60 cm from the display, and the room was normally lit. The test supervisor was present in the room for the whole duration of the recording but had minimum interaction with the participant during the actual recording or when the participant answered the questionnaire.

Before starting the experiment, the participant received written instructions (available in Finnish and in Russian) that gave a broad outline of what to expect. However, neither the contents of the documentary nor the exact goal of the experiment were revealed. The eye tracking equipment was calibrated with three-point calibration, and the calibration was verified at the start and the end of the recording. The eye movements were recorded only when the participant was watching the documentary. After seeing the video stimulus, the participant was handed the questionnaire and he or she could answer it at his or her own pace. In Experiment 2, the questionnaire was available for the participants in Finnish and in Russian and they could answer it in either of the languages. Typically the session took around 25 minutes in total.

To make the questionnaire data in Experiment 1 comparable with that of Experiment 2, the questions used for the analysis were the same, meaning that one image-related question and one subtitle-related question was omitted from the final analysis. To evaluate the effect of the omissions from the between-group analysis in Experiment 2, the statistical analysis was re-done with the omitted subtitle-related question, but this had no noticeable effect on the results. The questionnaire data was analysed with the χ^2-test, as in Experiment 1.

The gaze data was analysed with SMI BeGaze software (version 3.5). The analysis had to be done with the help of a process SMI calls "semantic gaze mapping", where gaze data from each recording is manually mapped to selected reference images. By default, the eye tracking glasses use their own scene camera recording as the stimulus video in which they map the gaze data. Mapping all recording data onto reference images via semantic gaze mappings essentially allows an aggregated data analysis of all participants as the analysis can be performed on the mapped reference images instead of the original recordings, each one of which includes data from only one participant. However, the BeGaze software currently does not allow videos to be used as reference stimulus in semantic gaze mapping, which meant that the mappings had to be done onto still screenshots of the documentary. This was not thought to pose a problem here, though, as the analysis is focused on the subtitles, which are a static element by nature. The advantage of the added accuracy of the eye tracking glasses weighted more when choosing the equipment for the experiment.

For the analysis of gaze patterns, the video was divided into scenes of variable lengths. Ten of these scenes were chosen for the analysis. The scenes were analysed as a whole, because the sample sizes in some of the scenes was too small to allow proper statistical analysis. Furthermore, there was no way to divide the scenes into meaningful groups, since all of the scenes consisted of similar audio-visual material (i.e. similar visual material and narration). The length of the chosen scenes varied from approximately 5 seconds to 30 seconds, with a total length of 1 minute and 58 seconds. This covered approximately one fourth of the stimulus video. The first minute and a half was left out of the analysis as an adjustment period. This was thought to give more natural data as the participants get more deeply immersed into the video and forget the experimental nature of the setting.

The image area was split into two areas of interest (AOIs): the subtitle AOI and image AOI. The eye tracking data of the two AOIs was compared statistically using the Wilcoxon rank sum test with continuity correction in the statistical software package R (version 3.1.0). The analysed metrics were average fixation duration, total dwell time, the number of glances, and fixation count. Average fixation duration is the summed duration of all fixations that land inside an AOI, divided by the number of those fixations. Dwell time equals the sum of all fixations and saccades starting from the first fixation and ending with the last fixation that lands an AOI, i.e. the time spent looking at a specific AOI. Average fixation duration and dwell time are reported in milliseconds. Glances mean the number of saccades that start from outside a specific AOI and end inside the AOI, i.e. the number of times the participant moves his or her gaze into an AOI. Essentially, the glance count helps us determine how often the subtitles were completely skipped. The fixation count is the total number of fixations that the participant made to a specific AOI. In this analysis, all zero values were omitted when analysing dwell times, average fixation durations and fixation counts, meaning that these were analysed only in cases where participants actually looked at the subtitle area.

The Wilcoxon rank sum test assumes that the compared data sets have homogeneous variances, which was achieved in the current data by transforming all dwell times and average fixation times with the common logarithm (log10). The tables below report the actual measured values rather than the transformed values. No transformations were necessary with glance and fixation count data.

2.2.3 Results

2.2.3.1 Questionnaire data
Figures 3 and 4, below show the relative number of correct answers in the ET-FI (eye-tracked Finnish) and ET-RU (eye-tracked Russian) groups in questions concerning the image and the subtitles respectively.

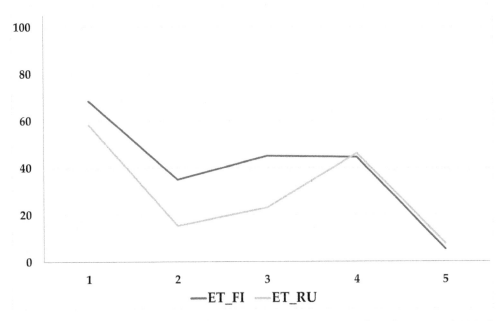

Figure 3: The percentage of correct answers in Finnish (ET-FI) and Russian (ET-RU) groups to the questions (1-5) concerning the image of the stimulus video.

Similarly to the results in Experiment 1, when both types of questions were analysed together, there was no statistically significant difference in the over-all performances of the two participant groups ($\chi^2(1)$ = 0.574, p = 0.449). In image questions (see Figure 3), the Finnish group got better scores in almost all questions, again as in Experiment 1, but this time the difference was much smaller and the difference in the overall score did not reach statistical signifi-cance ($\chi^2(1)$ = 1.24, p = 0.266). The results in the subtitle questions (see Figure 4) were more inconsistent across the individual questions, and the overall perfor-mance between the groups was similar and no statistical significance was evident ($\chi^2(1)$ = 0.028, p = 0.868). When each question was analysed individually, none of the questions had statistically significant difference between the groups, but one was close to the level of significance (question 14, $\chi^2(1)$ = 3.44, p = 0.064).

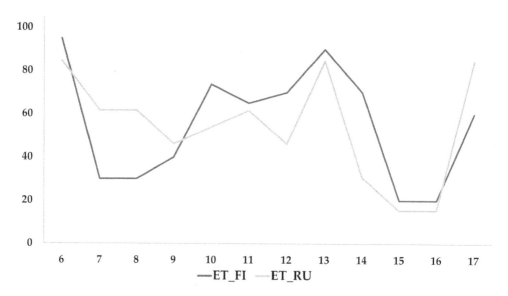

Figure 4: The percentage of correct answers in Finnish (ET-FI) and Russian (ET-RU) groups to the questions (6-17) concerning the subtitles of the stimulus video.

The stimulus and questionnaire were the same in both of the experiments, and this allowed a comparison of the Russian groups. In questions concerning the image, the difference was not statistically significant ($\chi^2(1) = 0.392, p = 0.531$, respectively), but in subtitle questions the difference was highly significant ($\chi^2(1) = 13.3, p < 0.001$). A comparison of the two Finnish groups revealed no statistical differences in either types of questions ($\chi^2(1) = 0.277, p = 0.600$ in image-related questions and $\chi^2(1) = 1.33, p = 0.248$ in subtitle-related questions). Since the Finnish groups were identical in terms of language skills and thus their performance was also expected to be identical, this shows that the different experimental settings did not have a significant impact on the results.

2.2.3.2 Eye tracking data   Table 1 shows the descriptive statistics for the number of glances into the subtitle area as well as the average dwell times, fixation durations, and fixation counts in the Finnish and Russian groups. The data shows that the Russian participants made significantly less glances to the subtitle area compared to the Finnish group ($W = 101932.5, p < 0.001$). They also skipped the subtitles completely in approximately 64% of the cases, while the Finnish participants skipped subtitles only in approximately 21% of the cases. Furthermore, when they looked at the subtitle area, the Russian groups' dwell times were shorter and fixation durations were longer compared to the Finnish groups, and

Table 1: Descriptive statistics for the number of glances, total dwell times (ms), average fixation duration (ms) and fixation count in the subtitle area for the Finnish and Russian groups.

	FI-ET				RU-ET		
	mean	sd	min	max	mean	sd	min
Glances	1.02	0.71	0.00	4.00	0.43	0.63	0.00
Dwell time (ms)	1129.17	811.75	99.30	4192.90	796.67	667.11	98.80
Average fixation duration (ms)	157.72	71.61	74.90	732.80	172.77	60.34	77.60
Fixation count	4.46	2.8	1.00	17.00	3.59	2.65	1.00

the Russian participants made fewer fixations to the subtitle area. All of these differences were statistically very significant (dwell time: $W = 63376.5, p < 0.001$; average fixation duration: $W = 38655.5; p < 0.001$, fixation count: $W = 60634.0, p < 0.001$). Standard deviations and ranges in the dwell times were quite large in both groups, indicating high variation between individual participants.

2.2.4 Discussion

The questionnaire data confirmed some of the findings that were discovered in Experiment 1. In Experiment 2, each group got a similar overall score in the subtitle questions although there was some variation between individual questions. Since the same information was available in both channels but the participants in the different groups could only effectively follow one of the channels, the results suggest that both types of verbal channels – the visual-verbal and audio-verbal channel – are equally effective as channels for acquiring information. Although this refutes Hypothesis 2, it also demonstrates that the subtitles area is as effective an information channel as the narration. This result is consistent with the results by Perego et al. (2010) and can be seen as further proof for the efficiency hypothesis (d'Ydewalle, Van Rensbergen & Pollet 1987).

Nevertheless, when the Russian group in Experiment 1 was compared to the Russian group in Experiment 2, the difference in scores was noticeable in favour of Experiment 1. This suggests that the possibility to follow both the narration and the subtitles gave them a significant advantage, and the redundant information channels enhanced the acquisition verbal of information, confirming Hypothesis 1. A similar effect has been found previously in studies examining language learning while watching subtitled films. Mitterer & McQueen (2009), for example, found out that watching a foreign language programme with intralingual subtitles (redundant audio and visual verbal channels) enhanced viewers' perception of speech.

The eye tracking data revealed, quite unsurprisingly, that the Finnish group made significantly more glances to the subtitle area than the Russian group. Furthermore, the Russian participants completely skipped over 60% of the subtitles, but when they did look at the subtitles they made longer but significantly fewer fixations than the Finnish participants. In comparison, Finnish participants skipped on average one of every five (21%) subtitles. The average fixation duration in normal reading of Finnish is approximately 250 milliseconds and the typical range is 100-500 milliseconds (Hyönä 1996), and the values are similar to normal reading of English (Rayner 1998). D'Ydewalle & De Bruycker (2007) reported adults' average fixation durations in standard (interlingual) subtitles as 178 milliseconds in one-lined subtitles and 179 milliseconds in two-lined subtitles. The averages reported here follow the same pattern: the average fixation durations of subtitles are shorter (157.72 milliseconds for the Finnish group and 172.77 milliseconds for the Russian group) than in normal reading. The reason for this is possibly the fact that television viewer's reading pace is dictated by the presentation time of the subtitles and, in cases where the viewer misses a subtitle, there is no way to go back. Thus the viewer has to adapt a faster reading strategy to make sure that he/she is able to read, and in cases of confusion possibly re-read, the subtitles.

Although in Experiment 2 the Finnish group performed better than the Russian group in most of the questions concerning the visual elements of the stimulus material, the difference did not reach statistical significance. In contrast, in Experiment 1 a statistically significant difference was found, with the Finnish group performing noticeably better than the Russian participants, so the results leave some room for speculation. Furthermore, the dwell times in Experiment 2 showed that the Russian group spent less time on the subtitle area than the Finnish group, by a very significant margin. It can be speculated that had the eye movements of the participants in Experiment 1 been tracked, the results would have been different. After all, the Russian participants in Experiment 1 understood the subtitles and most likely followed them more extensively than the Russian participants in Experiment 2.

Examined from another perspective, the difference in the dwell times suggests that, compared to the Finnish group, the Russian participants spent more time looking at the picture, and this was not reflected in the results of the questionnaire. On the contrary, in three of the five image-related questions the Finnish group got better scores than the Russian group. In other words, following subtitles did not have a negative effect on the Finnish groups' scores in the image questions, although reading subtitles drew the participants' attention away from the image. This indicates that reading subtitles is not a noticeable distraction from following the image, at least for people who are used to watching subtitled television programmes, which confirms Hypothesis 3. Perego et al. (2010) made the same conclusion, when they discovered that there was no noticeable trade-off in scene recognition and subtitle recognition when watching subtitled films. In contrast, in Experiment 1 the Russian group performed significantly worse in the image-related questions than the Finnish group. This suggests that the notion of unfamiliarity with subtitled material is at least partially the reason also for the contrasting results by Lavaur & Bairstow (2011), who found a trade-off effect of dialogue vs. visual comprehension with participants who had to rely on the subtitles in order to comprehend the dialogue of the film. Furthermore, they found that in the group who understood spoken dialogue, the visual comprehension score suffered from the presence of subtitles. The analysis in the present paper revealed no significant difference in the performances of the Russian groups in Experiment 1 and Experiment 2 in the image-related questions. This indicates that the subtitles had a similar effect on following the image for all Russian participants, no matter whether they could understand the subtitles or not.

One point worth mentioning is that although the Russian participants in Experiment 2 did not properly understand the language of the subtitles, they still looked at them in 40 percent of the cases. It has been shown that text seems to draw attention naturally in many contexts where it is presented with images, such as advertisements (Rayner et al. 2001; Rayner, Miller & Rotello 2008), and textual elements draw attention also in non-subtitled television material (Tosi, Mecacci & Pasquali 1997). The automaticity hypothesis introduced by d'Ydewalle, Van Rensbergen & Pollet (1987) stated that reading subtitles is an automated process, and it has been proven to be true even when viewers are not accustomed to watching subtitled programmes (d'Ydewalle et al. 1991). In the present study, the same effect was seen in a case where the participants did not even understand the language of the subtitles. Another explanation is possible here, though. The stimulus material of the present study was a short documentary, which naturally included facts such as numerical dates and important names. The participants knew before watching the video that the post-viewing questionnaire possibly required them to remember some of these facts. They were also often included in the subtitles and, as they were in a sense an inter-lingual element of the subtitles, the Russian participants could have spotted these facts from the text and used this as a memory-enhancing viewing strategy.

3 Conclusions

The aim of this study was to examine the acquisition of information from different information channels present in a subtitled television documentary. There were three hypotheses: 1) the access of two overlapping information channels should have a beneficial effect on the acquisition of information, 2) subtitles are a more efficient channel of information than narration, and 3) subtitles do not have a negative effect on the processing of image for viewers who are accustomed to watching subtitled films or television programmes. The questionnaire results of Experiment 1 and 2 confirmed Hypothesis 1, as in both experiments the access to both subtitles and narration improved the comprehension score, compared to the participants who only had access to one of the information channels. In contrast, Hypotheses 2 was refuted, as there was no visible difference in the performance of the two groups in Experiment 2 with subtitle-related questions. Hypothesis 3 was also confirmed, as the data in Experiment 2 showed no significant differences between the two groups in questions concerning the image, and the difference in Experiment 1 between the Russian and Finnish participants was statistically significant in favour of the Finnish group.

To summarize, the overlapping information channels can benefit viewers who can access both of them. The question of the effectiveness of the visual verbal and audio verbal channels remains open to debate, as no difference was found in the present study. It seems that subtitles are an effective way of translating foreign material, and those who are familiar with reading subtitles can also follow the image effectively despite following the subtitles. Nevertheless, it should be remembered that subtitles are bound by strict spatial and temporal constraints, and usually the original message has to be simplified and/or condensed as there simply is not enough time or space to include everything in the subtitles. Hence the role of the translator is an important one, because he or she ultimately decides what pieces of information are the most important to be conveyed and what can be left out. These experiments did not address the issue of emotional and aesthetic effects that subtitles have on the viewing experience, a viewpoint which could bring a new aspect to the discussion on audiovisual translation (AVT), especially when comparing dubbing and subtitling. Furthermore, in the stimulus material here the subtitles were done in accordance with the subtitling conventions, which ensured that the subtitles were formatted and paced so that they were easy to read and the participants had enough time to read them. In future, research into the validity of these conventions for cognition and reception could prove to be a beneficial approach in the study of audiovisual translating.

Acknowledgements

The author would like to thank Anna Petrova, from Petrozavodsk State University, for assistance in data collection, as well as the two anonymous reviewers for their valuable comments.

References

Brasel, S. Adam & James Gips. 2008. Points of view: Where do we look when we watch TV? *Perception* 37(12). 1890–1894.

Carroll, Patrick J, Jason R Young & Michael S Guertin. 1992. Visual analysis of cartoons: A view from the far side. In Keith Rayner (ed.), *Eye movements and visual cognition: Scene perception and reading*, 444–461. New York: Springer.

d'Ydewalle, Géry & Wim De Bruycker. 2007. Eye movements of children and adults while reading television subtitles. *European Psychologist* 12(3). 196–205.

d'Ydewalle, Géry & Ingrid Gielen. 1992. Attention allocation with overlapping sound, image, and text. In Keith Rayner (ed.), *Eye movements and visual cognition: Scene perception and reading*, 415–427. New York: Springer.

d'Ydewalle, Géry, Johan Van Rensbergen & Joris Pollet. 1987. Reading a message when the same message is available auditorily in another language: The case of subtitling. In J. K. O'Regan & A. Lévy-Schoen (eds.), *Eye movements: From physiology to cognition*, 313–321. Amsterdam: Elsevier.

d'Ydewalle, Géry, Caroline Praet, Karl Verfaillie & Johan Van Rensbergen. 1991. Watching subtitled television: Automatic reading behavior. *Communication Research* 5(18). 540–666.

Etemadi, Aida. 2012. Effects of bimodal subtitling of English movies on content comprehension and vocabulary recognition. *International Journal of English Linguistics* 1(2). 239–248.

Ghia, Elisa. 2012. The impact of translation strategies on subtitle reading. In Elisa Perego (ed.), *Eye tracking in audiovisual translation*, 155–182. Rome, Italy: Aracne Editrice.

Goldstein, Robert B., Russell L. Woods & Eli Peli. 2007. Where people look when watching movies: Do all viewers look at the same place? *Computers in Biology and Medicine* 37(7). 957–964.

Gottlieb, Henrik. 1998. Subtitling. In Mona Baker (ed.), *Routledge encyclopedia of translation studies*, 244–348. London: Routledge.

Hyönä, Jukka. 1996. Silmänliikkeet lukemisessa [eye movements in reading]. *Mieli ja aivot: Kognitiivinen neurotiede [Mind and brain: Cognitive neuroscience]* 1. Antti Revonsuo, Heikki Lang & Olli Aaltonen (eds.). 283–292.

Koolstra, Cees M. & Johannes W. J. Beentjes. 1999. Children's vocabulary acquisition in a foreign language through watching subtitled television programs at home. *Educational Technology Research and Development* 1(47). 51–60.

Latifi, Mehdi, Ali Mobalegh & Elham Mohammadi. 2011. Movie subtitles and the improvement of listening comprehension ability: Does it help? *The Journal of Language Teaching and Learning* 1(2). 18–29.

Lavaur, Jean-Marc & Dominique Bairstow. 2011. Languages on the screen: Is film comprehension related to the viewers' fluency level and to the language in the subtitles? *International Journal of Psychology* 46(6). 455–462.

Lee, Mina, Beverly Roskos & David R. Ewoldsen. 2013. The impact of subtitles on comprehension of narrative film. *Media Psychology* 16(4). 412–440.

Mitterer, Holger & James M. McQueen. 2009. Foreign subtitles help but native-language subtitles harm foreign speech perception. *PloS one* 4(11). e7785.

Paivio, Allan. 1986. *Mental representations: A dual coding approach*. New York: Oxford University Press.

Perego, Elisa. 2008. What would we read best? Hypotheses and suggestions for the location of line breaks in film subtitles. *The Sign Language Translator and Interpreter* 2(1). 35–63.

Perego, Elisa, Fabio Del Missier & Sara Bottiroli. 2015. Dubbing versus subtitling in young and older adults: Cognitive and evaluative aspects. *Perspective: Studies in Translatology* 23(1). 1–21.

Perego, Elisa, Fabio Del Missier, Marco Porta & Mauro Mosconi. 2010. Cognitive effectiveness of subtitle processing. *Media Psychology* 13(3). 243–272.

Rayner, Keith. 1998. Eye movements in reading and information processing: 20 years of research. *Psychological Bulletin* 124(3). 372–422.

Rayner, Keith. 2009. Eye movements and attention in reading, scene perception, and visual search. *The Quarterly Journal of Experimental Psychology* 62(8). 1457–1506.

Rayner, Keith, Brett Miller & Caren M. Rotello. 2008. Eye movements when looking at print advertisements: The goal of the viewer matters. *Applied Cognitive Psychology* 22(5). 697–707.

Rayner, Keith, Caren M. Rotello, Andrew J. Stewart, Jessica Keir & Susan A. Duffy. 2001. Integrating text and pictorial information: Eye movements when looking at print advertisements. *Journal of Experimental Psychology: Applied* 7(3). 219–226.

Tosi, Virgilio, Luciano Mecacci & Elio Pasquali. 1997. Scanning eye movements made when viewing film: Preliminary observations. *International Journal of Neuroscience* 92(1-2). 47–52.

Chapter 5

Monolingual post-editing: An exploratory study on research behaviour and target text quality

Jean Nitzke
Johannes Gutenberg University of Mainz in Germersheim

Technical developments and globalisation continue to accelerate the demand for translations. To improve efficiency and cost-effectiveness, organisations increasingly resort to machine translation and edit the machine translation output to create a fluent text that adheres to the given textual conventions. This procedure is called post-editing. Usually, post-editing refers to bilingual post-editing, which means that the editor can draw on the source text for the editing of the target text. However, machine translation output can also be edited without the source text, which is referred to as monolingual post-editing.

This study analyses monolingual post-editing products and processes of 24 participants – twelve semi-professional translators and twelve professional translators. In a set of experiments they were asked to translate from scratch, post-edit and monolingually post-edit two texts per task. The quality of the product, screen-recordings and eye-tracking data obtained during research are analysed for the monolingual post-editing task. Findings show that monolingual post-editing products are of similar quality in terms of superficial errors, such as grammar, spelling, etc., compared to translations from scratch and post-edited texts. However, many more content-based errors occur. Furthermore, different patterns can be found for monolingual post-editing processes in regard to research patterns and effort compared to the other tasks.

1 Introduction

Technical development and globalisation continue to increase the demand for translations. Despite economic and financial crises, more and more documents need to be translated, especially for internationally operating companies and organisations (Schmitt 2003; DePalma 2009). The emergence of new communication platforms – social media, discussion forums, blogs, etc. – also increases the

Jean Nitzke. 2016. Monolingual post-editing: An exploratory study on research behaviour and target text quality. In Silvia Hansen-Schirra & Sambor Grucza (eds.), *Eyetracking and Applied Linguistics*, 83–109. Berlin: Language Science Press. DOI:10.17169/langsci.b108.236

amount of available information in various languages. To improve efficiency and cost-effectiveness, organisations increasingly resort to machine translation (MT) and edit the MT output to create a fluent text that adheres to the given textual conventions (see O'Brien 2011; Elsen 2012). This procedure is known as post-editing. Usually, post-editing refers to bilingual post-editing, which means that the editor draws on the source text for the editing process. Similar to translation from scratch, the post-editor needs to be fluent in source and target language. Although translation from scratch and bilingual post-editing have common characteristics, and professional translators tend to be better post-editors than untrained individuals, the tasks differ in many aspects and some additional knowledge and skills are necessary for a translator to become a successful post-editor (see O'Brien 2002). Another possibility to edit the MT output is without the source text, which will be referred to as monolingual post-editing (MPE)[1] here. In MPE, the editor needs only to be fluent in the target language, as the source language is of no interest. Although the post-editor merely requires knowledge of one language it does not necessarily mean that the task is simplified, because (s)he has to rely on MT output and, depending on its quality, MPE can be a difficult undertaking.

While the opinion of professional translators on MT output is very subjective, scientific papers on (bilingual) post-editing often do not take the quality of the target text into consideration at all. Therefore, the following study will look at aspects that evaluate MPE products in regard to quality and research effort. First, §2 provides insights on related work. §3 briefly introduces the data set, methodology, and hypothesis. In §4, we will look at the finished MPE products and assess some error types that occurred in the target texts. Afterwards, the research effort in MPE will be analysed according to screen recording and eye-tracking data in §5. Research is a very time-consuming task when translating a text. Therefore, research effort should decrease in post-editing tasks. In §6, the conclusions of the analysis will be presented and the relationship between quality and research effort will be established. The paper ends with an outlook and suggestions for future work.

2 Related work

The non-scientific, professional translation community tends to have a low opinion of MT and post-editing and these topics have to be handled sensitively. Some

---

[1] Sometimes this editing task is also referred to as *blind post-editing* (e.g. Carl & Schaeffer 2013).

professional translators fear that their jobs are in danger or that they will be reduced to (in some opinions less enjoyable) editing tasks, and hence they fear that the public opinion of the profession *translator* will decrease (even more). However, uneducated opinions do not necessarily bear the truth, and prejudice towards the technology therefore surfaces. Events such as the 20th FIT World Congress in Berlin in July 2014 titled "Man vs. Machine? The Future of Translators, Interpreters and Terminologists", for example, were organised to bring translation practice and Translation Studies together, and to discuss the current state of MT and other technical aids including translation memory systems[2] that have become a necessity for professional translations over the course of the last decades. The title of the event already alludes to some of the aforementioned fears of professional translators and the industry as such. However, most translators who have sufficient knowledge about the technical developments probably will agree that these developments will not endanger job opportunities, but can assist the translator.

In a study conducted by the BDÜ[3] (BDÜ 2012), the use of Google Translate was assessed. It was concluded that the service might be a great online source for private communication, e.g. to make holidays preparations or as an aid while on holiday. However, for business communication, the free-to-use service is not suitable and is very quickly stretched to its limits. The BDÜ concluded that it can be embarrassing and bad for business to send business-related e-mails with mistakes or, even worse, run badly translated websites (see, e.g. ibid.: 9). Although the latter points are extremely valid, the study itself and the way it was conducted have to be treated very critically. Professional translators were asked to evaluate MT output for common language texts (newspaper articles about politics and menus/recipes), an excerpt of a manual belonging to a technical gadget, general terms and conditions of an online shop, and a business e-mail. Although different domains were covered, only one translator evaluated each text per language combination (German into English, Spanish, Polish, and Chinese) and each domain was represented by only one text. Furthermore, the texts created by the MT

---

[2] Translation memory systems store translation units (usually on a sentence basis) and suggest existing translations when the source unit is repeated in the text or another text. The translation unit does not need to be identical; usually a match of over 70% is sufficient for the system to suggest the stored translation (these matches are called fuzzy matches and the rate when a match is suggested can be customised). In modern translation memory systems many features are integrated, such as spell checkers, concordance search, terminology management systems, etc.

[3] Bundesverband für Dolmetscher und Übersetzer is one of the leading German professional associations of interpreters and translators with more than 7,500 members.

system were evaluated by a pointing system that is equal to the German grading system in schools (one to six, with one being the best mark and six the worst) in the following categories: correct content, grammar, spelling, idiomacy, and overall satisfaction with the text. The grades for the MT output texts were poor for most text types – except for the category spelling. However, this method of grading the texts is very subjective and does not represent what is actually important for MT output. The question of interest should rather be: When the MT output is used in a professional environment, how much effort does it take to transform it into a reasonable target text? In the BDÜ study, post-editing was acknowledged as a necessary step to arrive at a sensible target text (ibid.), but was not explained or referred to in detail. The benefits of the study are that it shows translators and potential clients that Google Translate is not almighty and that it cannot work without the help of a human translator. However, automatic translation is a rapidly developing branch and it has to be acknowledged how far the field has progressed, and that the systems do, in fact, work pretty well. Further, it should have been stated more explicitly that free-to-use online MT systems should not be compared to other MT systems, as many are far superior. Systems that are trained for one text domain and for one company will achieve much better results, assuming that they are used for the text type they were trained for: A system that was trained for household appliance manuals will probably not produce good translations for medical package inserts.

The necessity of hosting events such as the FIT conference and conduct studies like the one mentioned above shows that practising translators are interested in but also wary of some technical developments, and they might sometimes feel threatened by automatic translation systems. Therefore, it is necessary that Translation Studies objectively disclose both for translators as well as for clients the abilities and limitations of MT. Publications on (bilingual) post-editing often do not take the quality of the post-editing products into account, because they are more interested in the process than in the product and product quality was not (yet) crucial for the analysis in those studies (e.g. De Almeida & O'Brien 2010; Winther Balling & Carl 2014 and Bangalore et al. 2015). An assessment of the post-edited target text, however, would be very interesting and important in order to show the translation industry how post-editing can work and also where its limitations are. In addition, translation scholars might have a more critical and cautious attitude towards MT and the output of MT systems than computational linguists who develop the systems. While we agree that MT is better than no translation at all, MT output should not be overestimated. Scenario descriptions like the following should be treated with caution.

"We hypothesize that for at least some language pairs, monolingual poste-ditors with no knowledge of the source language can successfully translate a substantial fraction of test sentences. We expect this to be the case espe-cially when monolingual humans are domain experts with regard to the documents to be translated. If the hypothesis is confirmed, this could al-low for multi-stage translation workflows, where less highly skilled mono-lingual posteditors triage the translation process, postediting many of the sentences, while forwarding on the most difficult sentences to more highly skilled bilingual translators." (Schwartz et al. 2014: 191)

On the one hand, the quality of monolingually post-edited translation products is uncertain (unless someone who knows source and target language proof-reads the translation product). On the other hand, the more translators work on one text the more different styles get mixed and the less consistent and harder to read the text becomes. Further, translating single sentences is critical – as is sug-gested in the quote above that "highly skilled bilingual translators" (ibid.) shall take care of the more difficult sentences – because at least some inner-textual context might be necessary to translate a sentence correctly, especially when the sentence is rated as "difficult". It is also highly doubtful that a domain ex-pert is cheaper than an actual bilingual translator who is familiar with the do-main. Finally, it is necessary to keep the purpose of the translation in mind, which nowadays is a prerequisite in Translation Studies (e.g. most famously in the Skopos theory by Reiß & Vermeer 1984) and should be taken for granted for all post-editing situations as well.

A study conducted by Mitchell, Roturier & O'Brien (2013) deals in part with monolingual and bilingual post-editing results (English to German/French) that are evaluated by humans. The task for the participants was to evaluate whether the monolingual/bilingual post-editing product was better, the same, or worse (per segment, not the whole text) than the MT output according to the criteria *fluency, comprehensibility*, and *fidelity*. The results for the German data showed that bilingual post-editing products were improved more often (fluency 70.2%, compr. 64%, fidelity 56%) than MPE products (fluency 67.3%, compr. 57%, fidelity 43%). Nonetheless, the monolingual products were improved in all three criteria more often than stayed the same (fluency 20.4%, compr. 30%, fidelity 29%) or became worse (fluency 12.3%, compr. 13%, fidelity 28%).

"The results of this pilot study suggest that the monolingual set-up leads to similar results in terms of improvements and degradations in fluency and comprehensibility compared to the bilingual set-up. It also leads to a

greater number of improved segments for the bilingual set-up, with a considerable number of degradations, however." (Mitchell, Roturier & O'Brien
2013: 4)

The group of participants was rather small and the scores of the individual
participants varied a lot – especially for the German data. The same applies for
the time the participants needed to edit the texts. Therefore, the study did not
determine explicitly which task is more efficient and simultaneously provides the
best quality. However, these initial findings are striking and it is very interesting
that the participants performed so well in MPE, and that there were so many
degradations of quality in the bilingual post-editing tasks.

In a study published by Koehn (2010) the quality of MPE products was assessed
and compared to professional translations for the languages Arabic/Chinese into
English. Further, the difference between regular post-editing and interactive MT
– different translation options were suggested by the system – was investigated.
The participants could view the source text, but "[t]he translators had no knowledge of the source script" (ibid.: 540). Therefore, only some indications of numbers and punctuation could be taken from the source text. The assessment was
performed on sentence basis and the guideline for a correct sentence was "a fluent translation that contains the same meaning in the document context" (ibid.:
541). The monolingual product was compared to a reference translation by the
evaluators. Surprisingly, the professional translations were only evaluated as
correct in two thirds of the cases, which is far less than should be expected. The
monolingual post-edited sentences were correct in about one third of the cases
or less: Arabic → English 35%; Chinese → English 28% (ibid.). These results
could not be accepted for professional translations, but might be enough if the
target texts were used for information gathering or similar tasks.

3 Data set description and methodology

The study was conducted at the University of Mainz, Department for Language,
Culture and Translation Studies in Germersheim in 2012 on behalf of the Copenhagen Business School for their CRITT-TPR database (Carl 2012a; Carl & Schaeffer 2013) which collects translation process data. In the CRITT-TPR database,
data was collected for the same source texts but for different tasks, different target languages and with different tools[4]. Version 1.6 of the database was used for
the data analysis. In the sub-project from which the data at hand was taken, six

---

[4] http://sourceforge.net/projects/tprdb/ (last accessed 16th October 2015).

texts (newspaper articles and sociology-related texts) with different complexity levels had to be processed; the source language was English and the target language was German for all texts and tasks. The lengths of the source texts vary between 100 and 148 words. In total, 24 participants took part in the English-German subset, twelve of them professional translators (university degree and some professional work experience) and twelve semi-professionals (students of the university with only little professional experience). The participants were asked to translate two texts from scratch, bilingually post-edit two machine translated texts and monolingually post-edit two machine translated texts. The texts and tasks were permuted for each translator in a way that each text was translated and bilingually/monolingually post-edited equally often. Before and after the processing task, they had to complete questionnaires which dealt with general information about the participant, his/her attitude towards MT (in general and in regard to the MT output for the tasks), and self-estimation of their task performance. The MT output was produced by Google Translate (find more information on the dataset and the questionnaires in Carl, Gutermuth & Hansen-Schirra 2014).

The tasks were conducted in Translog II (Jakobsen 2011; Carl 2012b), a programme used to record the sessions, key-strokes, mouse activity and gaze data with the help of the Tobii TX300 eye-tracker, which also records the sessions, keystrokes, mouse activity and gaze data in Tobii Studio. There were no time restrictions and the participants could use the Internet freely as a research tool. Printed aids were not provided.

An experience vector was created to correlate research behaviour (and other phenomena) with experience. In the questionnaire prior to the experiments, the participants were asked how many years they had studied or had been studying translation at university and how many years of professional translation experience they had. This information was used and the experience vector was calculated using the following simple formula:

(1)   experience vector = years at university * 1 + years of professional experience * 2

As mentioned before, the participants were selected according to their status: 12 were students at the university, 12 had finished their studies and had professional work experience. However, those groups were heterogeneous in themselves: Some students already had some professional experience. By contrast, some professionals had only recently completed their studies and had only little professional working experience, while other professional translators had been working as freelance translators for more than 10 years. The experience vector, therefore, represents the experience of the single participants in more detail and can be adapted for correlation calculations. The minimum value for the experience vector is two (two years at university and no professional translation experience), the maximum value is 45 (five years at university and twenty years of professional translation experience). There was no further possibility for the participants to explain what they were doing in those years of professional translation, e.g. if they were working full-time or part-time as freelance or in house translators or if they translated on a daily/regular basis, etc. Therefore, the experience vector is the most that could be obtained from the data. It suggests that the participants gain more translation experience as practising translators than at university. The degree that students receive in Germersheim also includes linguistics and cultural studies. In addition, some courses are offered on translation theory, domain-specific knowledge or introduce scientific writing, etc. Hence, the years at university receive a lower value than years of professional experience.[5]

The following hypotheses will be explored in the analysis. First, a difference in quality is expected (§4): While superficial mistakes are made equally often in all three modes, content mistakes occur more often in MPE than in bilingual post-editing and translation from scratch, which would argue against MPE in professional translation tasks. Further, different Internet research patterns (§5.1) are predicted for MPE compared to the other two tasks. Regarding production times and gaze data for research-intensive words/phrases (§5.2), the parameters are expected to be higher in MPE than in the other tasks of the study. However, the parameter should be approximately the same when the words/phrases were not researched. Finally, as neither professional nor semi-professional translators are suspected to have extensive experience with MPE and MPE is suggested to be a very different task to translation from scratch, the translation experience of the participant is expected to have no significant influence on quality and research behaviour.

---

[5] The correlations in this article have been tested for different experience values as well with

   (i)   experience vector = years at university * 1 + years of professional experience * 1

   (ii) experience vector = years at university * 1 + years of professional experience * 1.5

   The correlation values and p-values naturally did change a little, but would not change the results, with only one exception in the first correlation for bilingual post-editing in §5.1, where the p-value was already close to the critical value .05. The correlation would in this case become significant. Hence, the experience vector may need further testing with larger data sets in future work.

4 Quality of the monolingually post-edited texts

Before analysis of the Internet research instances for the MPE tasks , the quality of the final texts will be assessed. Although the notion that the post-editor does not need to know the source language to edit MT output might be very tempting for clients, the quality of MPE output is very critical, because the post-editor cannot recognise content mistakes due to the lack of a source text.

Some of the problems that occurred on various occasions in the dataset were already discussed in Čulo et al. (2014). However, different behaviour was contrasted according to the tasks and according to how different tasks influence local and global translation strategies. Single examples were discussed in regard to idiomacy, lexical consistency, word order, and preserving semantic content. While MPE performed well in the first three examples, it failed in the example of preserving semantic content. The content component is naturally essential for successful translation products and will therefore be analysed in more detail.

In Schäfer (2003) error categories are introduced that were established at SAP AG to develop a standard post-editing guide. At the time the paper was published, four different MT systems were used at SAP AG for different languages. The four error categories introduced are: *Lexical errors, syntactical errors, grammatical mistakes*, and *mistakes due to defective source texts*. The latter did not occur in the six source texts in this study, which needs to be a given in an experimental setting. However, this is an important aspect when technical texts are translated in practice (Horn-Helf 1999; 2007). Not only translators but also technical writers often have to deal with time pressure and tight deadlines. Therefore, defects in the source text are quite common in technical documentation. Another aspect is that MT output was analysed in Schäfer's study, while this study will focus on mistakes in the final target texts. Therefore, syntactical mistakes were not included, because they appear less often in the post-edited text than in MT output and some syntactical structures could be categorised as bad style, which is not included in this analysis. However, a few categories have to be added, such as spelling mistakes, which occur only occasionally in MT but quite often in human translation. Further, the key-logging system Translog II does not include an automatic spell checker – a tool, which is standard in most of the environments that translators work in, such as word processing programmes and translation memory systems. Interestingly, especially in the other tasks (translation from scratch and bilingual post-editing) many spelling mistakes occurred, which were probably typing mistakes rather than ignorance in terms of how the word is spelled correctly. This indicates that translators tend to rely on the spell checker and are not used to focussing on these kind of mistakes.

In the first subsection, the focus will be on superficial error categories, because they can be applied for all three tasks of the study and are equally wrong in all tasks as they did not occur due to the post-editing guidelines, or resulted from the missing source text in the MPE task. The following error categories were established: *Spelling, grammar, punctuation, spaces,* and *lexical mistakes*. The latter only concern lexical errors that can be detected without consulting the source text, which applies for the rest of the error categories as well. In general, it is expected that these superficial errors occur as often in MPE as in translation from scratch and in post-editing.

The second subsection will analyse content mistakes that occurred in MPE. This will include the following categories: *Addition of information, missing information,* and *wrong information* (problematic lexical choices/content/etc.). Conclusively, those mistakes can only be discovered when the source text is taken into consideration, because a fluent text was created on the surface. Content mistakes are expected to occur much more often in the MPE task than in other tasks because of the missing source text.

The differentiation between mistakes that are obvious even without (superficial mistakes) or only with the source text (content mistakes) is essential in MPE, because the translator cannot be blamed for the content mistakes as they only result from a misinterpretation of the MT output. Superficial mistakes, however, could have been discovered or avoided. Conclusively, a high number of content mistakes in the MPE tasks argues against MPE in professional translation tasks, because they do not reflect the skills of the translator but the difficulty of the task itself.

Two of the MPE sessions had to be dismissed because of technical problems with the key-logging software. The remaining 44 monolingual post-edited products were assessed for superficial and content mistakes. The results will be briefly compared with the results of the translation from scratch and bilingual post-editing tasks, for which 43 and 48 sessions could be assessed.

4.1 Superficial mistakes

On average, the participants made 1.3 superficial mistakes (SD: 1.27) per text, which is slightly lower than for the other tasks (translation from scratch: mean: 1.47, SD: 1.28; post-editing: mean: 1.56, SD: 1.36). The mistakes that occurred most often were *grammar* and *lexical* mistakes (for both: mean: 0.48; SD: 0.76). There is no significant correlation between experience of the participants and number of mistakes[6] (r_τ = .01, p= 0.91). The results coincide with what was initially expected: The amount of superficial mistakes are almost the same in all three tasks. Interestingly, the experience of the participant has no influence either.

4.2 Content mistakes

MPE products are suspected to be prone to content mistakes, depending on the quality of the MT output, which would be the main disadvantage in comparison to post-editing with the source text and an editor who knows the source language. In this section, we will first discuss some examples of content mistakes from the dataset and their degree of inaccuracy and then the main focus will be put on the overall dataset. Some content mistakes might originate from an incorrect MT (the mistakes were created by the MT system and the translator did not realise the mistake), while others might have arisen from a misinterpretation of MT output by the translator. Hence, the mistakes were created by the translator or by a combination of MT and translator influence.

4.2.1 Example of MPE products with content mistakes

When the content is transmitted incorrectly, the information in the text/of the communication is distorted or lost. Some content mistakes in monolingual PE were less serious than others, because they did not change the whole content of the sentences/text and did not change the overall message of the text. In the following, some examples of content mistakes in the dataset will be introduced (Table 1 & 2) and discussed.

The minor content mistakes neither deliver the message of the text correctly nor create a different tone in the text or drive the context in a different direction. In example (1), the perspective is wrong. The source text says that the victims of the murders could have been considered a burden to the hospital staff in general. However, the monolingual post-edited target text says that he (the murderer) considered them a burden, which is probably true as well, but is not entirely what the source text stated. In example (2), it does not say in the target sentence that the gesture was meant to rattle the Chinese Government. So, one aspect of the source sentence is missing. However, the interpretation that the gesture was much-noticed could be correct as well and – for what it is worth – it was probably Spielberg's intention to elicit strong reactions from the media, etc., concerning his behaviour.

---

[6] In the following correlation tests, the data are not normally distributed and hence, the non-parametric Kendall's Tau test is used.

Table 1: Examples of minor content mistakes through MPE

Source sentence	Monolingual post-edited target sentence	Back-translation of target sentence
Minor content mistakes		
(1) All of them could be considered a burden to hospital staff.	Alle von ihnen soll er als eine Last für das Krankenhauspersonal empfunden haben.	He apparently considered all of them a burden to the hospital stuff.
(2) In a gesture sure to rattle the Chinese Government, Steven Spielberg pulled out of the Beijing Olympics [...].	In einer vielbeachteten Geste reiste Steven Spielberg von den Olympischen Spielen in Peking ab [...].	In a much-noticed gesture, Steven Spielberg left the Beijing Olympics [...].

The major content mistakes on the other side deliver information that is definitely not correct. Example (3) states that the Sudanese Government was invited to a conference on crimes against humanity, while the source text actually stated that one minister of the government was charged with crimes against humanity. Therefore, the information in the target sentences is definitely incorrect and delivers the wrong, rather positive picture about the Sudanese Government. In the last example (4), the lexical miss-decisions make the target text absurd, because the target text readers would get confused as to why a hunter-gatherer society should have tourist guides or clerks at all (especially as the first sentence of the text explains that hunter-gatherer societies are nomadic).

4.2.2 Results

On average, the participants made 2.23 (SD: 1.18) content mistakes per monolingual post-edited text, which is far more than in the other two tasks (mean: 0.46, SD: 0.71). When separated by task, there are even less content mistakes in bilingual post-editing (mean: 0.30, SD: 0.51) than in translation from scratch (mean: 0.61, SD: 0.83). One reason for this might be that the participants translate more freely

Table 2: Examples of major content mistakes through MPE

Source sentence	Monolingual post-edited target sentence	Back-translation of target sentence
(3) China, which has extensive investments in the Sudanese oil industry, maintains close links with the Government, which includes one minister charged with crimes against humanity by the International Criminal Court in The Hague.	China, das umfangreiche Investitionen in der sudanesischen Ölindustrie getätigt hat, pflegt enge Beziehungen mit der Regierung, die auf ein Ministertreffen zum Thema Menschenrechtsverletzungen des Internationalen Strafgerichtshof in Den Haag geladen sind.	China, which has effected extensive investments in the Sudanese oil industry, maintains close links with the government, which was invited to a ministerial meeting on crimes against humanity organised by the International Criminal Court in The Hague.
(4) As a result, full-time leaders, bureaucrats, or artisans are rarely supported by hunter-gatherer societies.	In Jäger-Sammler-Gesellschaften sind daher Touristen-Führer, Büroangestellte und Handwerker selten vertreten.	As a result, tourist guides, office workers, and artisans are rarely featured in hunter-gatherer societies.

in translation from scratch and therefore might transmit the information incorrectly. The mistake group that occurred most frequent in MPE was *wrong information* (Mean: 1.95, SD: 1.24), while *addition of information* (Mean: 0.11, SD: 0.32) and *missing information* (Mean: 0.16, SD: 0.43) hardly occurred – the category *wrong information* includes many more mistakes than the other two groups. Furthermore, there is no significant correlation between experience of the participants and the amount of content errors that occurred in the target texts (r_τ= -.06, p= .6).

4.3 Interpretation of error analysis

The large number of content mistakes can be explained easily by the missing source text. The translator depends on the MT output and interprets it in his/her own way. They guess blindly what the correct meaning of the text might be and either they get it right or they do not. Interestingly, the participants do not get better at "guessing" the more translation experience they have. This also applies to superficial mistakes: Although it would have been reasonable to expect that more experienced translators make less superficial mistakes, there is no significant correlation between experience and number of mistakes. This might be explained with the help of two arguments. First, the post-editing tasks were new to most participants. Second, the editor in Translog II is probably an unfamiliar work environment for professional and semi-professional participants, which was additionally not equipped with a spell checker.

The superficial errors occurred less often in MPE than in the other two tasks. One possible explanation could be that the participants were more focused on the surface of the text due to missing context. The main task in MPE is to correct and improve the text, while translation production is the main task when translating from scratch (and partly when bilingually post-editing MT output as well). Therefore, the correct transcoding of content into the target text becomes much more important in translating from scratch and bilingual post-editing. According to the key-logging data, many more tokens were typed in the translation from scratch session – on average 1117.2 tokens – while on average only 305.7 tokens were typed in the MPE task. Logically, more typing errors can occur when more text is written.

The number of mistakes (no matter which error category) and the amount of experience do not correlate for MPE. It might be expected that the more experienced a translator is the less mistakes (s)he makes. The MPE task was (probably) very unfamiliar for all participants (the questionnaires revealed that only $^1/_3$ of the participants had experience in bilingual post-editing), no matter how much translation experience they had. Therefore, their translation experience did not help to create a correct monolingual post-edited product. This could indicate that MPE is not (particularly) related to the task translation from scratch.

5 Research behaviour

The research the participants conducted in the MPE tasks was quite different from the other tasks, because they did not have the source text as a reference.

Nonetheless, different online aids can help to improve the target texts and and/or disentangle the MT output and were used accordingly by the participants.

Due to technical problems during the recording, only 43 sessions (20 professionals and 23 semi-professionals) can be used to assess the screen recording in regard to research effort. In 51.2% (60% professionals, 43.5% semi-professionals) of all MPE sessions, no Internet research was conducted at all, while no research was conducted in only 19% (33.3% professionals and only 4.8% semi-professionals) of the sessions in the human translation task. Therefore, monolingual editors used Internet research far less than in other tasks, which indicates that it is a different problem they are dealing with.

The remaining sessions that contain Internet research will be analysed in the following. In the first part, the screen recording results will be assessed: How often was research necessary? What kind of sources were used? And in the second part, the focus will be on production times and specific eye-tracking data: How long did the production of the unit take and how long was the unit looked at?

5.1 Screen recordings

The Internet was consulted for research in 163 instances during all MPE sessions. On average, 3.8 research instances (SD: 5.9) were conducted per session. However, quite often one word/phrase did require more than one research instance, e.g. different online dictionaries were consulted or – especially in the MPE task – one word/phrase was first back-translated into English and then one or more of the English suggestions were looked up in the online dictionaries. Therefore, the number of problematic words/phrases that required research was much lower (mean: 1.4; SD: 2.0). Conclusively, one problematic word/phrase needed 2.7 look-up instances (SD: 4.2), which is much higher than for translation from scratch (mean: 1.5; SD: 1.2) and post-editing (mean: 1.5, SD: 1.5). This shows that the research effort per problematic word/phrase is much higher than for the other tasks, which seems reasonable because of the missing source text. However, the values of research instances per session (TFS mean: 8, SD: 6.5; PE mean: 4.4, SD: 4.3) and problematic words/phrases per session (TFS mean: 5.3, SD: 4; PE mean: 2.8, SD: 2.6) are much lower than for the other tasks. To sum up, less research is needed for MPE, but when research is necessary it is more elaborate.

In MPE, the correlation between experience vector and total research effort ($r_\tau = -.17$, p= .14) as well as the correlation between experience vector and words/

phrases researched per session ($r_\tau = -.2$, p= .1)[7] is not significant, while the values correlate significantly for translation from scratch ($r_\tau = -.34$, p> 0.01/$r_\tau = -.34$, p> .01) and in one case for bilingual post-editing ($r_\tau = -.21$, p= .07/$r_\tau = -.28$, p= .02). In both translation from scratch and bilingual post-editing, the data correlates negatively, which means that the more experience a translator has the less often (s)he researches per overall text and per word.

Different sources were used and categorised as follows (see also Figure 1): Bilingual dictionaries (101 instances – this group includes all sources that provide bilingual information to avoid creating too many subgroups), monolingual dictionaries (four instances), synonym dictionaries (four instances), MT systems (18 instances), encyclopedic websites (eleven instances), search engines (21 instances), and news websites (four instances).[8]

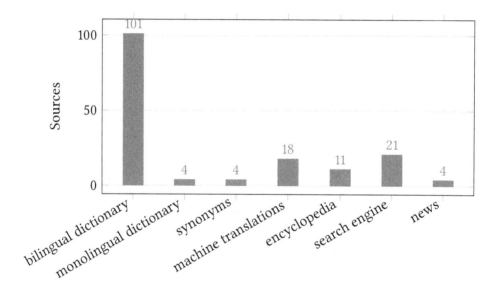

Figure 1: Sources for research

In all three tasks, bilingual dictionaries were used most frequently for research. However, in MPE bilingual dictionaries were used the least often. In addition, MPE is the only task in which the translators used MT. This was caused by the missing source text, which was generated by automatic back translation of the

---

[7] In the following paragraph, the first specification in the brackets will refer to the correlation between experience vector and total research effort. The second will specify the correlation between experience vector and words/phrases researched per session.

[8] The three participants who used news websites did read related articles and did not find the original texts.

MT output. Interestingly, all translators, who used MT as a research tool, back-translated the target text with Google Translate, although they did not know that the MT output had been originally generated by Google Translate. Maybe the back-translation would have been less helpful if the participants had used another MT system.

5.2 Eye-tracking data

The focus in this section is on the processing effort of the words/phrases that were researched most often in all tasks. The words/phrases that were researched in the Internet in at least four sessions were chosen for the analysis in order to ensure some validity. Further, some words/phrases were excluded for different reasons, e.g. last words of headlines, because some gaze data may have been assigned to the last words of the headline although the gaze was somewhere else in the rest of the line after the line break. Words/phrases that occurred more than once in the text were excluded as well, because it cannot be determined for certain where in the text the word/phrase became problematic. After excluding these research instances, a total of 28 words/phrases can be analysed.

However, as already discussed in §5.1, there was less research in MPE than in bilingual post-editing and translation from scratch. Conclusively, some of the words/phrases were not researched in MPE and will be excluded as well. Finally, one word had to be excluded due to technical problems in the eye-tracking data (see Table 3 for the amount of remaining words per text).

In two instances, the word/phrase was not researched during bilingual post-editing either, e.g. "insistence" in text two was looked up five times in the translation from scratch session, but never in the post-editing sessions. The machine translated "insistence" with "Beharren", which is an acceptable translation for the word in the context of text two and therefore reduced the research effort in the post-editing tasks. Conclusively, the MT system made the translation process in those instances easier, because it was a high research effort word in the translation from scratch task but did not have to be researched when the text was machine translated.

Table 3: Number of words/phrases that were taken into consideration per text, excluding those that were not researched in monolingual editing.

	Text 1	Text 2	Text 3	Text 4	Text 5	Text 6
No. Words/Phrases	0	2	3	1	3	2

When phrases were looked up, the gaze data for the whole phrase was taken into consideration and not only for the words that were actually looked up. For example, in the dependent sentence "which includes one minister charged with crimes against humanity by the International Criminal Court in The Hague" some translators researched "Criminal Court", "International Criminal Court", "International Criminal Court in The Hague", etc. The production time and gaze data of the whole phrase "International Criminal Court in The Hague" was taken into consideration, even if only "Criminal Court" was looked up, so that the different research instances are comparable, no matter how the translator decided to gather information on the phrase.

The CRITT-TPR database contains tables with key-logging and eye-tracking data for each translator and task (see Carl & Schaeffer 2013 for a detailed explanation of the various parameters). To compare the data, two parameters were chosen, one concerned with production time (*Dur*) and one with gaze data (*GazeT*):

(2) **Dur**: Duration of unit production time [...]
     GazeT: Total gaze time on target text unit [...] (ibid.: 22)

Dur and GazeT include all instances in which the target word/phrase was produced or looked at. Therefore, they can be used to compare the mental effort of the particular unit in the overall session. This is important because the word/phrase may not have been considered problematic at first glance. Nor can be implied that the word/phrase became unproblematic after the research instance or the (first) production of the target word/phrase. In future analyses of the translation from scratch and bilingual post-editing task, the parameter for the gaze on the source text will be taken into consideration as well. However, as the source text is missing in this task, data on the source text will obviously not be taken into account.

The mean values for Dur (Table 6) and GazeT (Table 7) will be compared for the whole dataset with the MPE data in the next paragraphs. No statistical evaluation will be conducted for the data, because n is very small for the research instances per word/phrase task (see Tables 4 and 5). In a follow-up study the number of participants would have to be increased to find statistically significant differences between the different tasks. It is expected that *Dur* and *GazeT* are higher for researched words/phrases in MPE than the other tasks. The parameter should be approximately the same when the words/phrases were not researched.

In six out of ten instances, the mean for the production of the word/phrase is higher in MPE than the mean duration for all tasks when the word/phrase was researched. The mean duration for MPE is only higher in one instance than in

Table 4: Occurrences of the most researched words/phrases in the complete dataset and in MPE

Words/phrases	Sessions (MPE sessions)	Sessions with research on the word/phrase	Sessions with no research
below-inflation	20 (7)	5	15
cut interest rates	20 (7)	7	13
rattle	21 (7)	11	10
halt	21 (7)	5	16
Khartoum	21 (7)	6	15
incentives	22 (7)	10	12
associate	21 (8)	10	11
exposure	21 (8)	9	12
bureaucrats	21 (7)	9	12
full-time leader	21 (7)	8	13

all tasks when the word/phrase was not researched. These results were expected and indicate that the production time for research intensive words/phrases is higher in MPE than in other tasks. One reason could be that, in general, the MT output first has to be deleted in post-editing and then the new translation is inserted, while there is only the production of the word/phrase in translation from scratch. Further, due to the missing source text, the translator might be insecure with his/her solution and therefore needs more time to produce the unit than in bilingual post-editing. To prove these hypotheses, more research instances and hence more participants would be necessary.

The mean for GazeT of the word/phrase is higher in MPE than the mean duration for all tasks in two out of ten instances. This is true for both cases when the word/phrase was researched and when it was not. This means that more gaze is spent in only 20% of the research-intensive words/phrases, no matter whether the word/phrase was researched in the Internet or not. Therefore, the processing of research-intensive words/phrases seems to be equally or even less problematic than in other tasks, which is contrary to what was expected. Especially when we take into consideration that processing also takes place while reading the source

Table 5: Occurrences of the most researched words/phrases in the complete dataset and in MPE

Words/phrases	Sessions (MPE sessions)	Sessions with research in MPE (n)	Sessions with no research in MPE
below-inflation	20 (7)	1	6
cut interest rates	20 (7)	2	5
rattle	21 (7)	2	5
halt	21 (7)	1	6
Khartoum	21 (7)	1	6
incentives	22 (7)	2	5
associate	21 (8)	2	6
exposure	21 (8)	4	4
bureaucrats	21 (7)	4	3
full-time leader	21 (7)	2	5

Table 6: Mean Dur for the particular word/phrase for all research instances, all non-research instances, MPE research, and MPE non-research

Dur	All research	All non-research	MPE research	MPE non-research
below-inflation	7369.2	5114.9	8533	3737.3
cut interest rates	8622.6	1400.8	1069	1227
rattle	10796.5	2817.7	5070.5	3975
halt	10421.2	940.9	42869	235.5
Khartoum	13478.8	3330.8	14291	215
incentives	2756.8	5712.2	4867	2851
associate	1753.5	777.6	876	383
exposure	9798.3	193.8	24008.5	0
bureaucrats	1015.7	1281.6	1336.3	0
full-time leader	20733.8	3884.3	2160.5	2764.2

Table 7: Mean GazeT for the particular word/phrase for all research instances, all non-research instances, MPE research, and MPE research

Dur	All research	All non-research	MPE research	MPE non-research
below-inflation	2671.6	10123	2160	8775.7
cut interest rates	7395.9	5431.9	3797.5	3659
rattle	14353.5	4764.1	1455	1083.8
halt	7217.6	2052.5	1325	1657.5
Khartoum	2330.5	1329.6	1634	158.3
incentives	2484	4388.3	406.5	1398.2
associate	1578.1	2256.5	3221.5	1706.7
exposure	2759.3	2943.2	1067.5	424.8
bureaucrats	11018.7	5249.2	14563	6288.7
full-time leader	6062.9	7167.8	3178	7814.4

text in translations from scratch and bilingual post-editing. As mentioned above, n for research instances in MPE is too small to conduct any valuable significance tests. Hence, the discussed results indicate a tendency, but a much larger dataset would be needed to test the hypothesis accordingly.

6 Conclusion

The quality of MPE products is not comparable to translations from scratch or bilingual post-edited texts. While the surface of the text is good and even fewer superficial mistakes occurred in MPE than in other tasks of the dataset, the content of the products is error-prone and is not acceptable. The target texts often contain (slightly) different meanings than the source texts and are therefore not suitable for many translation purposes, especially if the translation is intended for publication. For information gathering, however, the target texts could be used in most cases.

Research behaviour in MPE is different than in other tasks. No Internet research was used at all in over half of the sessions. In those sessions that contained Internet research, fewer words/phrases were researched. However, when research is necessary it is more elaborate, because the participants use more research instances to find a solution for a difficult word/phrase. The main sources of research were bilingual dictionaries in MPE as well as in the other tasks. However, in relation to other sources, it was used less frequently. Further, only mono-lingual editors used MT systems as a resource to create a source-text-like text.

The production times of research intensive words tend to be higher in MPE than in other tasks. Contrary to what was expected, the eye-tracking data for MPE do not indicate more gaze behaviour than in other tasks. However, the dataset is too small to draw any statistically significant solutions.

There is no statistically significant correlation between experience and research behaviour. That might indicate that MPE is only partly related to translation and that translators do not benefit much from their translation experience. Making sense out of an error-prone text that may or may not be the correct interpreta-tion due to lacking reference material (in regular translation situations the source text) is not what translators are trained to do, which was also indicated in the retrospective questionnaire.

In the retrospective questionnaire, we asked the participants how satisfied they had been with their post-editing tasks. The participants could choose from five answers, each choice was given a value that will be added in brackets: highly satisfied (two points), somewhat satisfied (one point), neutral (no point), some-what dissatisfied (minus one point) and highly dissatisfied (minus two points). The mean of the added values indicates which tendency the participants had in judging their results. The professionals were quite critical about their work and were not satisfied (mean: -0.68, SD: 1.43) with their monolingual post-edited tar-get texts. The semi-professionals were neither satisfied nor dissatisfied with their work (mean: 0.08, SD: 1.08). The satisfaction with the bilingual post-editing task was higher; however, professionals (mean: 0.18, SD: 1.25) were still more critical about their bilingual post-editing product than semi-professionals (mean: 0.67, SD: 0.89). This low satisfaction with the MPE tasks could be a sign that the par-ticipants were rather frustrated with the task. The task was new to (most of) the participants and they could not use the problem-solving strategies they use in translation from scratch. One remaining question is how much influence experi-ence in MPE would have on the final target text. Maybe some strategies that are unique for MPE would be developed after some experience and the task would a) produce better target texts and b) would be less exhausting/frustrating.

7 Future work and outlook

Unfortunately, the questionnaires did not include questions about the transla-tors' proof-reading experience. Usually, translators have to proof-read other translation products or regular texts quite often, but some (professional) translators might do proof-reading as one of their main work task, while others might just do it occasionally. Semi-professional translators might have different experience in proof-reading as well. For bilingual post-editing, it has already been agreed that it is more than mere proof-reading of MT output (e.g. O'Brien 2002). However, due to the lack of a source text, monolingual post-editing might be closer to traditional reviewing/proof-reading than bilingual post-editing, even if the MT system often produces completely different mistakes and makes more mistakes than a human translator would. Therefore, there might be a significant correlation between revising/poof-reading experience and MPE, which could be explored in a follow-up study.

The amount of data in this study is critical to explore research behaviour and research patterns that are different to those in bilingual post-editing and translation from scratch. In particular, there was far too little eye-tracking data to draw significant conclusions on likeliness or differences between the different tasks. Additionally, every participant monolingually edited only every third text and not every participant looked up the same words/phrases. Therefore, a much bigger group would be necessary to evaluate significant relations.

Research behaviour in MPE should also be investigated for other text types, as translating newspaper articles and other texts in general language is not common in professional translation practice. An online survey (Hommerich & Reiß 2011) conducted by the BDÜ reported that 49% of the members that participated in the study (in total 1570) specialised in the field "Industry and Technology (general)", 45% in "Law and Administration", 41% in "Economics, Trade, and Finances", 25% in "Medicine and Pharmacy", and 23% in "Information Technology". Only few translators specialised in fields that might require the use of general language like "Culture and Education" (13%), "Sports, Recreation, and Tourism" (10%), or "Media and Art" (9%), although most of these fields might require domain-specific language and terminology as well. As a consequence, the results of domain-trained MT systems would probably be of better quality than the MT output of Google Translate.

MPE is a noble goal for MT. The notion that the user does not need to know the source language and that only a few corrections concerning grammar and syntax are necessary to create a functioning text is very appealing, but from a Translation Studies perspective this will not become a reality in the near future. Of course, the success of MT output is extremely dependent on the purpose of the target text. When the text is intended for publication, a source text will be necessary for the translator to ensure that the content of the target text is correct. In stylistically diverse texts, translation from scratch might still be preferable to post-editing, but even in domain-specific texts which would be proof-read by monolingual domain experts, the risk of material or personal damage is too high to not consider the source text. Nonetheless, MPE is a task that will remain interesting in research, e.g. to evaluate MT output.

In the future, MT output might become so accurate that MPE becomes an option for professional translation tasks. As soon as this goal is achieved – at least for some translation purposes – it would be reasonable to consider integrating MPE into translation training in a similar way to bilingual post-editing (O'Brien 2002), because the data indicate the task is very different from translation from scratch and bilingual post-editing. However, bilingual post-editing needs to be integrated into university curricula first. Bilingual post-editing courses also have the advantage that students might become aware of the dangers and difficulties of MPE by themselves or might be made aware of these by the instructor, so that they can make the right decisions if they ever encounter a MPE job and can consult clients in regard to the MPE task.

References

Bangalore, Srinivas, Bergljot Behrens, Michael Carl, Maheshwar Ghankot, Arndt Heilmann, Jean Nitzke, Moritz Schaeffer & Annegret Sturm. 2015. The role of syntactic variation in translation and post-editing. *Translation Spaces* 4(1). 119–144.

BDÜ. 2012. Mensch ./. Maschine – Ergebnisse der BDÜ-Untersuchung zur Qualität der Übersetzungen durch Google Translate. Pressedossier. Berlin. http : / / www . bdue . de / uploads / media / 2796 _ BDUe _ _Pressedossier _ MenschMaschine_10.2012.pdf, accessed 2016-08-18.

Carl, Michael. 2012a. The CRITT tpr-db 1.0: A database for empirical human translation process research. In *AMTA 2012 Workshop on Post-Editing Technology and Practice (WPTP-2012)*, 9–18.

Carl, Michael. 2012b. Translog-II: A program for recording user activity data for empirical reading and writing research. In *LREC 2012*, 4108–4112.

Carl, Michael, Silke Gutermuth & Silvia Hansen-Schirra. 2014. Post-editing machine translation – a usability test for professional translation settings. In Aline Ferreira & John W. Schwieter (eds.), *Psycholinguistic and cognitive inquiries in translation and interpretation studies*, 145–174. Newcastle upon Tyne: Cambridge Scholars Publishing.

Carl, Michael & Moritz J. Schaeffer. 2013. The CRITT translation process research database v1. 4. http://bridge.cbs.dk/resources/tpr-db/TPR-DB1.4.pdf, accessed 2016-08-18.

Čulo, Oliver, Silke Gutermuth, Silvia Hansen-Schirra & Jean Nitzke. 2014. *The influence of post-editing on translation strategies.* Sharon O'Brien, Laura Winther Balling, Michael Carl, Michel Simard & Lucia Specia (eds.). Newcastle upon Tyne: Cambridge Scholars Publishing.

De Almeida, Giselle & Sharon O'Brien. 2010. Analysing post-editing performance: Correlations with years of translation experience. In *Proceedings of the 14th annual conference of the European association for machine translation, St. Raphaël, France*, 27–28.

DePalma, Donald A. 2009. Chancen der Globalisierung. *MDÜ* 2. 10–13.

Elsen, Harald. 2012. Postediting – Schreckgespenst oder Perspektive. *MDÜ* 4. 16–21.

Hommerich, Christoph & Nicole Reiß. 2011. Ergebnisse der BDÜ-Mitgliederbefragung.

Horn-Helf, Brigitte. 1999. *Technisches Übersetzen in Theorie und Praxis.* Tübingen: Francke.

Horn-Helf, Brigitte. 2007. *Kulturdifferenz in Fachtextsortenkonventionen: Analyse und Translation: Ein Lehr-und Arbeitsbuch.* Vol. 4. Karlsruhe, Germany: Peter Lang.

Jakobsen, Arnt Lykke. 2011. Tracking translators' keystrokes and eye movements with Translog. In Cecilia Alvstad, Adelina Hild & Elisabet Tiselius (eds.), *Methods and strategies of process research*, 37–55. Amsterdam: John Benjamins.

Koehn, Philipp. 2010. Enabling monolingual translators: Post-editing vs. options. In *Human language technologies: The 2010 annual Conference of the North American Chapter of the Association for Computational Linguistics*, 537–545. Association for Computational Linguistics.

Mitchell, Linda, Johann Roturier & Sharon O'Brien. 2013. Community-based post-editing of machine-translated content: Monolingual vs. bilingual. In *Machine Translation Summit XIV*, 35–43. European Association for Machine Translation. European Association for Machine Translation.

O'Brien, Sharon. 2002. Teaching post-editing: A proposal for course content. In *6th EAMT Workshop Teaching Machine Translation*, 99–106. Manchester, U.K.

O'Brien, Sharon. 2011. Towards predicting post-editing productivity. *Machine Translation* 25(3). 197–215.

Reiß, Katharina & Hans J. Vermeer. 1984. *Grundlegung einer allgemeinen Translationstheorie* (Linguistische Arbeiten 147). Tübingen: Niemeyer.

Schäfer, Falko. 2003. MT post-Editing: How to shed light on the 'unknown task'. Experiences at SAP. In *Proceedings of EAMT-CLAW-03*, 133–140. Dublin, Ireland: European Association for Machine Translation.

Schmitt, Peter A. 2003. Berufsbild. In Mary Snell-Hornby, Hans G. Hönig, Paul Kußmaul & Peter A. Schmitt (eds.), *Handbuch translation*, 1–5. Tübingen: Stauffenburg.

Schwartz, Lane O. B., Timothy Anderson, Jeremy Gwinnup & Katherine M. Young. 2014. Machine translation and monolingual postediting: The afrl wmt-14 system. In *Proceedings of the Ninth Workshop on Statistical Machine Translation*, 186–194.

Winther Balling, Laura & Michael Carl. 2014. *Production time across languages and tasks: A large-scale analysis using the CRITT translation process database.* Newcastle upon Tyne: Cambridge Scholars Publishing.

Chapter 6

Investigating cognitive effort in post-editing: A relevance-theoretical approach

Fabio Alves, Karina Sarto Szpak
Universidade Federal de Minas Gerais, Brazil

José Luiz Gonçalves
Universidade Federal de Ouro Preto, Brazil

Kyoko Sekino, Marceli Aquino, Rodrigo Araújo e Castro, Arlene Koglin, Norma B. de Lima Fonseca
Universidade Federal de Minas Gerais, Brazil

Bartolomé Mesa-Lao
Copenhagen Business School

This paper presents the results of an experimental study that investigates the influence of cognitive effort on post-editing tasks from a relevance-theoretic perspective (Wilson 2011). Using two short scientific texts, we compare post-editing processes in two different machine translation web-based workbenches, namely interactive machine translation (IMT) and standard, non-interactive machine translation (MT). The relevance-theoretic concepts of conceptual and procedural encodings (Wilson 2011) and the methodology developed by Alves & Gonçalves (2013) to assess cognitive processes in the course of translation tasks are used as the framework for data analysis. Sixteen professional translators performed interactive and non-interactive post-editing tasks in random order, their processes were recorded with the aid of a Tobii T60 eye tracker. Data were collected with the CASMACAT workbench and results pointed to the following conclusions: (1) as it has been found in human translation (Alves & Gonçalves 2013), the percentage of edits related to procedural encoding is significantly higher than that related to conceptual encoding; (2) interactive post-editing requires less cognitive effort, as shown by the average and median fixation duration which was statistically lower when using the

Fabio Alves, Karina Sarto Szpak, José Luiz Gonçalves, Kyoko Sekino, Marceli Aquino, Rodrigo Araújo e Castro, Arlene Koglin, Norma B. de Lima Fonseca & Bartolomé Mesa-Lao. 2016. Investigating cognitive effort in post-editing: A relevance-theoretical approach. In Silvia Hansen-Schirra & Sambor Grucza (eds.), *Eyetracking and Applied Linguistics*, 109–142. Berlin: Language Science Press. DOI:10.17169/langsci.b108.296

interactive system. As a way of conclusion, the paper reflects on these results and their implications for the development of interactive machine translation platforms for post-editing.

1 Introduction

It has been widely acknowledged that the aim of machine translation is to produce high-quality translation as well as speeding up translation tasks and enhancing the cost-effectiveness of this process. In order to meet the increasing demand for translations, machine-translation technology has been largely adopted by language service providers worldwide, although human translators are still required to post-edit machine-translated outputs (De Almeida 2013: 17).

Actually, to achieve high-quality products, there is a need for professional human interaction either before or after the machine has processed the data (O'Brien 2004: 3). Intervention before the machine processes is called *pre-editing* and it occurs at the source-language level. The main objective of pre-editing is to reduce time and effort for post-editing by implementing a number of strategies such as text manipulation. Intervention after the machine process is called *post-editing* and it occurs at the target-language level to correct possible errors in the MT output (Mesa-Lao 2013).

In general, post-editing (henceforth PEd, to be differentiated from the procedural encoding acronym [PE] used throughout this paper) consists in correcting or editing texts that have been translated from a source language into a target language by a machine translation system. A useful definition can be found in Somers (2001), who also comments on the value and importance of the PEd process to achieve an understandable text from a machine translation output:

> As automated translation still has many limitations even nowadays, the corrections made by human linguists remain indispensable to make machine-translated texts more understandable and accessible to readers. (Somers 2001: 138)

According to Krings, who introduces one of the most extensive works on PEd research, "the question of post-editing effort is the key issue in the evaluation of the practicality of machine translation systems" (Krings & Koby 2001: 178). He proposes that PEd effort can be measured on three levels: temporal, technical and cognitive. Temporal effort refers to the time taken to post-edit a particular text; technical effort refers to deletions, insertions and text re-ordering; cognitive effort deals with the extent and type of cognitive processes that the translator needs to apply on a machine translation output, i.e., the amount of effort expended in a PEd task (O'Brien 2006). In this work we focus our attention on the third level proposed by Krings, that is, cognitive effort, seen from a relevance-theoretic perspective (Sperber & Wilson 1986), wherein the concepts of conceptual, procedural and hybrid encodings underpin the framework for data analysis. These concepts will be further explored in the next section.

Relevance Theory (RT henceforth) postulates that human cognition is guided by relevance, i.e., essentially seeking information that is relevant for obtaining as many cognitive effects as possible. In other words, RT is based on the premise that our cognition seeks to achieve the greatest cognitive effects with the minimum necessary processing effort. According to Wilson (2011: 72), the human cognitive system tends to "follow a path of least effort in looking for implications; test interpretations in order of accessibility, and stop when your expectations of relevance are satisfied".

In this sense, post-editing tasks seem to fit RT assumptions since, according to Loffler-Laurian (1984; 1996), one of the main characteristics of PEd would be the quicker turnaround (in comparison to human translation from scratch), and its focus on corrections that are essential and relevant. In accordance with Loffler-Laurian's work, in the past few years there has been increasing evidence for productivity gains when professional translators have post-edited machine translation output. Empirical research has demonstrated that PEd can lead to higher productivity. A significant number of studies have compared PEd against translation from scratch. Results from these studies indicate that PEd processes can be very efficient, showing productivity gains of 80% (Plitt & Masselot 2010; Skadiņš et al. 2011; Pouliquen, Mazenc & Iorio 2011; Federico, Cattelan & Trombetti 2012).

Even with the significant research about the process of post-editing tasks – e.g. Guerberof Arenas (2012), O'Brien (2006), Fiederer & O'Brien (2009), Depraetere (2010), Plitt & Masselot (2010), De Sousa, Aziz & Specia (2011), Specia et al. (2009), Specia (2011) – there is more to know about its usefulness and the influence on the translators' decision-making processes.

Considering these studies, this paper aims at contributing to PEd research by investigating processing effort, drawing on the concepts of conceptual, procedural and hybrid encodings over two post-editing tasks performed with the aid of the CASMACAT workbench, a statistical machine translation system, used in conjunction with a Tobii T60 eye tracker.

To that end, this article is divided into five sections, including this Introduction. In §2, we outline the theoretical underpinnings, with special attention dedicated to the concepts of conceptual, procedural and hybrid encodings (Moeschler

1998; Wilson 2011; Alves & Gonçalves 2013). In §3, we discuss our methodological framework. In §4, we turn to the statistical analysis, explaining the main distinction between effort spent on interactive and non-interactive post-editing tasks. Finally, we end the article with discussions and concluding remarks in §5.

2 Theoretical underpinnings

This section describes and discusses some concepts from Relevance Theory (Sperber & Wilson 1986) and their application to the problems concerning cognitive effort in post-editing experimental tasks.

Sperber and Wilson's *Relevance: communication and cognition* (1986/1995) outlines a very productive and powerful framework for describing and explaining human communicative interactions from two important scientific domains: pragmatics and cognitive studies. While postulating the principle of relevance, the authors introduced a consistent way of integrating these two domains and shed new light on issues concerning language processing as the core of human communicative interactions. They revisited and reformulated key concepts such as context, mutual knowledge, cooperation, code, inference, and representation, among others, into a very coherent and parsimonious framework.

In this section, we will present some concepts from Relevance Theory required to develop the analyses and discussions on the problems we have focused on.

2.1 The principle of relevance

RT postulates its principle as a mechanism that produces a balance between processing effort and cognitive effects: "[...] in any given inferential process, the human being's cognitive environment searches for the generation of the maximum cognitive effects possible while spending the minimum processing effort necessary to achieve this end" (Alves & Gonçalves 2013: 109). Therefore, the principle of relevance regulates effort and effect relations in inferential processing in order to enhance human beings' cognitive environments. Thus, this guarantees one's cognitive adaptation to one's physical and social environments. In short, it is a kind of economic and adaptive principle.

For instance, if a piece of inferential processing demands too much effort, and in turn gives insufficient or very few relevant results (or cognitive effects), it will probably be interrupted or even abandoned, i.e., the person will tend to give up going ahead with that specific piece of processing. On the other hand, if inferential processing tends to achieve many effects, the human cognitive system will indicate when the quantity and quality of those effects are enough/adequate, determining that it has reached optimal relevance, which is a kind of cognitive "satisfaction". Therefore, this principle prevents the cognitive system from spending unproductive or unnecessary processing effort.

More specifically, RT accounts for the unfolding of human inferential processes through the following sequence:

---

processing effort →
[ostensive-inferential behaviour + (cognitive environment + mutual manifestness)]
→ **cognitive effects**

Figure 1: The relevance-theoretic comprehension procedure (Adapted from Alves & Gonçalves 2003: 6)

Figure 1 schematically summarizes which aspects are required for a certain amount of processing effort to generate a number of cognitive effects. Whenever the ostensive-inferential condition is achieved, inferential communication is about to take place, that is to say, when two interacting individuals (a communicator and a hearer) share a certain level of cognitive representations (i.e., when they reach some level of mutual manifestness) in their cognitive environments, they are ready to communicate. A communicative process is expected to generate as many cognitive effects as possible in the hearer's cognitive environment. This presumption of relevance (generating the maximum of effects possible with the minimum of effort necessary) is another requirement for communication to take place. Therefore, in ostensive-inferential communication, humans try to avoid unnecessary processing effort when there is no benefit in terms of cognitive effects.

Next, we will discuss how this principle can be productive for translation-related issues.

2.2 Interpretive resemblance

When applied to translation, the principle of relevance is expanded to take into account the concept of *interpretive resemblance*. This concept has been developed in the RT framework from the notion of *interpretive use* of mental representations, a second-order level of representations, as opposed to *descriptive use* of mental representations, a first-order level of representations. In short, *descriptive use* establishes a correlation between real or fictional world phenomena/objects and mental representations, while *interpretive use* correlates pairs of mental representations.

For instance, when someone says

(1)   Mary is coming to the party.

the hearer in this situation will build up in her cognitive environment a representation of an event or state of affairs in the real world or in an imaginary world. In this example, there is a case of *descriptive use* of language, connecting a mental representation to an event (whether real or not).

On the other hand, if someone says

(2)   I don't believe Mary is coming to the party.

the hearer, in this second situation, will have not only to represent a state of affairs or event from the external world in her cognitive environment, but also that it is represented as not true in the speaker's cognitive environment. Here, there is a case of *interpretive use*, i.e., the hearer creates a second order mental representation aiming at resembling the speaker's mental representation behind that utterance.

Building on this notion of *interpretive use*, Gutt (1991) defined translation as the search for *interpretive resemblance* between corresponding utterances, one in the source language and the other in the target language. Gonçalves (2003) expanded the focus of that definition, applying it to the concept of translation unit (TU) as the entity to be individually interpreted, transferred and compared in the course of the translation process. According to Gonçalves (2003), this process is aimed at maximizing *interpretive resemblance* between a source-text translation unit and its target-text counterpart. This *interpretive resemblance*, in line with the principle of relevance, determines that the production of contextual or cognitive effects from the interpretation of the source-text translation unit should overlap, as much as possible, with those effects found in the production/interpretation of the counterpart target-text translation unit. The effects from both source and target language TUs are represented by the respective sets of explicatures (the explicit semantic content of a linguistic input) and implicatures (the less explicit and progressively implicit content, i.e., the inferred implications of that input).

To build up *interpretive resemblance* in translation, the translator is expected to *meta-represent* his/her audience's cognitive environment. Meta-representations are higher order representations that allow the communicator, among other things, to simulate mentally his/her audience's inferential context (as well as that of the source text author and source text audience) in order to achieve the most adequate cognitive effects through the production of appropriate stimuli in the target language.

In the process of post-editing, post-editors are guided by the meta-representation that the final product has to be good enough for the purposes agreed upon with the client (either a fast, light or a full, human-quality post-edited translation) necessarily spending less time than translating from scratch (cf. Carl et al. 2011; Sanchis-Trilles et al. 2014). As it will be discussed in §2.4, it is very important that post-editors bear in mind the crucial relation between time (effort) and quality (effects) for the success of post-editing tasks, reducing time (and eventually processing effort) to a minimum possible and increasing quality (related to cognitive/contextual effects) to the maximum required for the PEd modality in focus or almost as good as a human professional translation.

Therefore, especially in fast, light PEd, translation acceptability by the target audience will be more flexible. Considering that one of the goals in PEd in this modality is to achieve a good enough target text in the shortest time possible, processing effort commonly spent on stylistic refining will tend to be avoided or reduced to a minimum since the main goal in that particular task modality is, in most cases, to offer, as soon as possible, a reasonably understandable product to its audience.

While translating from scratch, translators tend to generate a number of implicatures for a certain problematic translation unit. As Alves & Gonçalves (2007) pointed out, the more expert the translator is, the greater the number of implicatures s/he will be able to generate for a problematic unit in order to choose the one that will best suit a relevance-oriented processing in his/her audience's cognitive environment – a textual input that may generate the maximum (and the most precise) cognitive effects possible with the minimum processing effort necessary to accomplish the task.

In PEd, however, due to higher time pressure demands, the translator/post-editor is expected to save time and cognitive effort as the machine translation (MT) system generates a first version of the target text. Thus, still following the principle of relevance, s/he will try to find a good enough solution (always considering the modality of PEd agreed upon for the task – fast or full), calculating its effects on the audience's cognitive environment and, then, accepting integrally or partially the raw MT output. More specifically, while post-editing a machine translation output with the help of an interactive system (IMT), the post-editor will be offered some optional solutions for a specific problem in case he decides to change something in a translation unit. These solutions offered by the IMT system will change the post-editors' reading purpose since, from an initial change, all the rest of the output is automatically changed, leaving to the post-editor the decision of either reading for revision or for post-editing.

In this regard, Lykke Jakobsen & Jensen (2008) investigated the effects of the type of task (reading for understanding, for translating, for sight translation, and for written translation) on eye movements and concluded that the reading purpose had a clear effect on eye movements and on gaze time. Thereby, interactive systems are expected to show an effect on eye movements related to post-editing processes by reducing the cognitive processing effort demanded during the output revision, as it will be postulated in one of our hypotheses and discussed in §4.

2.3 Conceptual and procedural encodings

As we have shown in the preceding subsections, the main focus of RT is on inferential processes, as they are decisive for an individual's cognitive improvement and adaptation to his/her physical and social environment. However, some studies building on RT (e.g. Moeschler 1998; Blakemore 2002; Wilson 2011; Alves & Gonçalves 2003; 2013) have focused on encoding/decoding as the initial, triggering (and therefore essential) stage of the cognitive processing for verbal communication. Moeschler (1998) postulates the distinction between conceptual and procedural encodings.

In Relevance Theory, a major distinction is made between two types of linguistically encoded information: conceptual information and procedural information (Wilson & Sperber 1993). The conceptual/procedural distinction is motivated both linguistically and cognitively.

1. Conceptual information is mainly encoded within lexical categories (Noun, Verb, Adjective), that is, categories which define open lexical classes. Procedural information is encoded within non-lexical categories (negation, tenses, determiners, connectives, certain adverbials), that is, categories which define non-open morphological classes. Thus the conceptual/procedural distinction covers mainly the distinction between lexical and non-lexical categories.

2. The cognitive motivation for the procedural/conceptual distinction is the following: conceptual information is information through which mental representations are accessible, whereas procedural information encodes instructions relative to how mental representations must be processed. (Moeschler 1998: 1)

On the one hand, as conceptual encodings refer to, say, more concrete entities, with extra-linguistic references, as nouns, adjectives, verbs, mainly, they are subject to conscious access. On the other hand, procedural encodings, encompassing morph-syntactical rules and restrictions on language structure, are not usually amenable to conscious processing, except indirectly, through meta-cognitive reflection.

As Alves, Gonçalves & Szpak (2014) explain, the function of conceptual expressions (i.e., open lexical categories, such as nouns, adjectives and verbs) is to convey conceptual meaning which is propositionally extendable and contributes to expanding the inferential processing of an utterance whereas the function of procedural expressions is to activate domain-specific cognitive procedures (i.e., morph-syntactic constraints in utterance processing) and contributes to constraining the inferential processing of these same utterances. Relevance Theory assumes that the conceptual-procedural distinction guides inferential processing. (Alves, Gonçalves & Szpak 2014: 155)

Besides conceptual and procedural encodings, Alves & Gonçalves (2013), drawing on Wilson's (2011) arguments, postulated a third category of encoding for a lexical item – the hybrid encoders (HE). This third category is found in lexical items including both encoding functions, which encompass most words since exclusively conceptually encoded items are rather the exception than the rule in terms of linguistic encoding.

The studies of Alves (2007) and Alves & Gonçalves (2003) have corroborated the principle of relevance while showing a relation between processing effort and cognitive effects in translation. The authors have also shown that there is an important distinction between the role of conceptual and procedural encodings. However, those were small-scale studies and only offered qualitative results. Alves & Gonçalves (2013) used a larger sample to build on the previous relevance-theoretic findings and corroborated them by means of statistical analyses. Using key-logged data to map instances of conceptual and procedural encodings onto micro/macro translation units (Alves & Vale 2009; 2011), Alves & Gonçalves (2013) concluded from their results that problems related to procedural encodings demand more processing effort both in direct and inverse translation tasks.

2.4 Post-editing, relevance and encoding

As we mentioned above, post-editing aims at offering an acceptable and intelligible target text for a certain audience in a specific context within a significantly shorter period of time than that spent in a human translation. And as in any translation process, the aim is maximizing interpretive resemblance between source and target texts. Thus, in PEd as well, a post-editor seeks for a product (a post-edited target text) that will optimally resemble the source text, or that will resemble it in relevant aspects.

In this respect, depending on the type of post-editing agreed between client and translator, there will be more or less acceptability and tolerance for minor formal and stylistic inaccuracies in the post-edited text. In Relevance Theory terms, the target text receptor will be more inclined and ready to overcome some small imperfections, accepting a certain increase in the processing effort to achieve the cognitive effects that will lead him/her to optimal interpretive resemblance. In this case, the reader accepts that a post-edited product demands slightly more effort to be processed but supposedly results in the expected (and approximately the same amount of) effects as in human translation – reader and client accept this state of affairs since the deadline is usually much shorter and the cost significantly cheaper. Therefore, in PEd "the demand of faster and cheaper translations increases" (Aziz, Koponen & Specia 2014: 171). It is important to highlight that, according to the principle of relevance, there are limits for this acceptability – the cognitive effort demanded from the audience may not surpass a certain limit and the effects are expected to optimally (or minimally in relevant aspects) resemble those in the source text.

Taking into account Alves & Gonçalves (2013) results, that procedural encoding (PE) edits are more prevalent than conceptual encoding (CE) edits in human translation, and that machine translation systems have been developed to facilitate human translation tasks, it is important to ask if this prevalence will be kept or modified in PEd.

Some highly optimistic approaches to PEd say so. Green, Heer & Manning (2013), for instance, report that the use of basic post-editing tools by bilingual human translators improves translation quality in comparison to texts produced by bilingual human translators working without the assistance from machine translation and post-editing tools. Some sophisticated interactive interfaces, like translation memories (TM), machine translation (MT), computer-assisted MT, statistical MT (SMT), interactive translation prediction (ITP) approach (Langlais & Lapalme 2002; Casacuberta et al. 2009; Barrachina et al. 2009), online learning approach (Ortiz-Martınez et al. 2012), active learning approach (González-Rubio & Casacuberta 2014), and multitask learning approach (de Souza et al. 2014), may also provide benefit, especially with regard to post-editors' productivity, i.e., reduction of time, cost and processing effort.

2.5 Hypotheses

1. In the IMT condition, there will be fewer instances of editing events (total, CE, PE) than in the MT condition, since the interactive system is expected to provide more optional and possibly better solutions as soon as the post-editor starts editing a certain unit, thus preventing him/her from proceeding with that specific piece of editing.

2. As in Alves & Gonçalves (2013), there will be more instances of procedural than conceptual related edits in PEd, both in the MT and the IMT condition. We expect that machine translation will more likely solve and/or reduce problems related to conceptual than to procedural encodings, leaving procedural related problems to be solved by post-editing procedures.

3. In the IMT condition, the average and median duration of an eye-fixation will be shorter than in the MT condition, since the interactive system is expected to reduce processing effort compared to the non-interactive system. Drawing on Lykke Jakobsen & Jensen (2008), we expect that in IMT there will be more reading for checking and revising than for writing and editing, which is more frequent in MT.

4. Considering PE and CE edits, as interactive machine translation is expected to reduce cognitive effort, the average fixation duration per edit (CE and PE) will be shorter in the IMT condition than in the MT condition.

Based on these hypotheses, the main goal of this paper is to investigate the impact of conceptual, procedural and hybrid encoding edits over the cognitive effort patterns observed in the interactive and non-interactive post-editing processes by Brazilian professional translators in the English-Portuguese language pair.

3 Methodological framework

This section is divided into two subsections. First, we introduce the experimental design; secondly, we present the methodology for data analysis, giving special attention to the procedures for annotating post-editing process data.

3.1 Experimental design

Sixteen Brazilian translators, with at least five years of professional experience, were asked to post-edit, into Brazilian Portuguese (L1), two source texts in English (L2) about the clinical results of two different pharmacological products, Hycamtin and Protaphane (see Appendix). Before starting the task, participants were instructed through a brief with a detailed description on the procedures.

Data were collected using the CASMACAT workbench (Cognitive Analysis and Statistical Methods for Advanced Computer Aided Translation), a statistical machine translation (SMT) system developed by the CASMACAT project team, in conjunction with a Tobii T60 eye tracker, at the Laboratory for Experimentation in Translation (LETRA) in Brazil. In order to remove the effects of participants' heterogeneity, a randomized block design, in which the plots form a set of eight replicated 2x2 Latin squares, was used. Thereby, source texts were post-edited in a random order, as well as the type of workbench configuration, non-interactive machine translation (MT) or interactive machine translation (IMT).

According to Alabau et al. (2013), in the IMT approach, a fully-fledged machine translation engine is embedded into a post-editing workbench allowing the system to look for alternative translations whenever the human translator corrects the output offered by the SMT.

For a given source sentence, the SMT system automatically generates an initial translation that is checked and edited by the participant. The SMT system then proposes a new completion taking into account the corrections. These steps are repeated until the whole input sentence has been correctly translated. In this way, the system produces a suitable prediction according to the text that the participant is writing. Figure 2 shows the IMT workbench in which the grey colour represents the suitable prediction, the red dots indicate eye movement paths, the acronym ITP (Interactive Translation Prediction) identifies the type of workbench and T→ (Start Translating) shows the target text in the selected language of interest. The user can also assign a different status to a segment, for instance, "TRANSLATED" for finished ones or "DRAFT" for the ones he/she wants to review later.

Figure 2: Example of IMT prediction workbench

In the MT approach, on the other hand, the SMT system produces full target sentences, or portions thereof, which can be accepted or edited by the participant. However, in this case, when an error is corrected, no predictions are offered by the SMT. Figure 3 shows the MT workbench, in which the acronym PE stands for post-editing and one can observe that no predictions are offered while the participant is editing the segment.

Figure 3: Example of MT workbench

Before the post-editing tasks, participants were asked to fill out a questionnaire in order to collect data about their profiles as professional translators, as well as their previous experience in post-editing. Eye calibration was also performed before the tasks, according to the instructions provided in the Tobii T60 user's manual.

Building on Alves, Gonçalves & Szpak (2012) and Alves & Gonçalves (2013), the methodology was refined in order to investigate the relevance-theoretic conceptual/procedural distinction in the post-editing process. We have thus correlated the edits performed in the text segments to their respective visual activity in selected areas of interest (AOIs). The next subsection presents the methodological steps taken to achieve that end.

3.2 Procedures for data analysis

First, each MT and IMT post-editing task was filtered in order to avoid the overlapping of eye-activity data (for detailed information on filtering eye tracking data, see Alves, Gonçalves & Szpak 2012). Thus, we created a set of scenes containing only eye tracking data directly related to an individual segment at a given time. In order to clarify this methodological procedure, it is necessary to explain how the SMT system operates.

The CASMACAT workbench is a web-based CAT tool with an entry point in a web page that the users log into using a personal user name and a password. Once the user has been logged in and selected an assignment, the text opens up in the actual CAT tool. The source text appears in segments on the left and the target text on the right.

In this study, we worked with 17 segments for the text about Protaphane and 19 segments for the text about Hycamtin. Once the post-editing tasks were randomized, this difference between the number of segments in each text was not a problem in terms of data analysis. Differences in text size and complexity will be explored in other studies on the same data.

In order to access all the segments provided by the CASMACAT workbench, participants had to use the scroll bar, which can be a problem when recording gaze activity with the Tobii T-60 eye-tracker, as participants tend to keep their focus of attention on the centre of the screen, causing data overlap, as can be seen in Figure 4.

Figure 4: Example of segment data overlap

On the left, we can observe the area corresponding to the first segment, displayed in white, and the area corresponding to the second segment displayed in red, with the brackets representing the extent of the visual activity area applied to each segment, where the overlapping is visible.

Thus, based on Alves, Gonçalves & Szpak (2012) methodology, all participants' data had to be filtered. Using Tobii Studio replay mode, we selected each ST/TT segment and a set of 17 scenes were created for the text about Protaphane and a set of 19 scenes were created for the text about Hycamtin. This can be seen in Figure 5. At the bottom of the screen, it is possible to visualize the process time line shown in the selection bar, right under it one can see the scenes created according to the segments provided by the CASMACAT workbench.

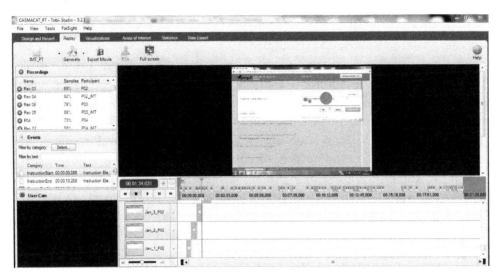

Figure 5: Filtering individual eye tracking data segment by segment

As a second step, AOIs were created in order to extract statistically relevant information on gaze activity. Using Tobii Studio 3.2.3, we obtained measures for fixation count and their duration. Drawing on Sjørup (2013: 105), we applied a fixation duration threshold of 180 milliseconds in order to discriminate acceptable data from non-acceptable data. The software generated an Excel file containing data for all participants in both tasks, which serves as the basis for our statistical analyses.

As a third step, in our attempt to map instances of conceptual, procedural and hybrid encodings onto post-editing process data, we had to annotate the editing procedures (deletions, insertions, clause reordering) performed in each textual segment. To that end, the videos recorded while participants performed the post-editing tasks were analysed and a frequency table containing number and type of encodings was created.

We based our annotation on the categories proposed by Alves & Gonçalves (2013), wherein the total number of conceptual encodings is equivalent to the sum of lexical editing procedures and complex phrasal structure editing procedures {[l] + [p]}; the total number of procedural encodings is equal to the sum of a morph-syntactic editing procedures and complex phrasal structure editing procedures {[m] + [p]}; and the total number of hybrid encodings is equal to the editing procedures where a lexical item includes both encoding functions [p].

Therefore, the editing procedures performed in the complete set of 36 segments were annotated individually with reference to the input offered by the SMT systems. The data coming from this annotation were correlated to the eye tracking data, so we could analyse the cognitive effort patterns applied to each type of workbench configuration, (MT) and (IMT).

Thus, the number of edits on all types of encodings performed in each segment were analysed according to four different types of methodological analyses: i) the number of encoding edits per task, that gives an overall impression of which condition, MT or IMT, demands higher number of edits related either to conceptual or procedural encoding, ii) the number of eye fixations per condition, that presents the total number of fixations allocated during a post-editing task, iii) fixation duration per condition (MT and IMT), that discusses how cognitively demanding the different post-editing workbench systems are, and iv) average/median fixation duration per condition, that discusses the difference between the two post-editing conditions in terms of cognitive effort.

4 Analysis and discussion

4.1 Results

The results presented in this section are mainly comparisons of the number of edits related to CE, PE and HE encodings and the eye tracking data variables, such as fixation counts, fixation duration and average/median fixation duration between conditions. Initially, we will present the results of edits on encodings in the MT and the IMT condition. Next, we will analyse the results regarding visual activity. Finally, we will assess the correlation between edits and visual activity.

4.1.1 Edits in encodings

The edits related to conceptual, procedural and hybrid encodings were annotated and counted individually as shown in Table 1.

Initially, we characterize our data on encodings in order to make clear the relation between CE, PE and HE. Before our detailed analysis, we realized that hybrid encodings had an extremely low occurrence, less than 1% of all edits. Thus, in this study we only analyse edits in CE and PE, distributing HE to CE and PE equally (cf. Alves & Gonçalves 2013). The total number of CE and PE is summarized in Table 2.

Looking at overall editing-related results, contrasting the two conditions, that is, MT vs. IMT, without distinguishing the texts, we found no difference in the

Table 1: Number of edits per participant concerning conceptual, procedural and hybrid encodings in MT and IMT conditions.

Participants	Text	MT CE	PE	HE	Text	IMT CE	PE	HE
P02	PR	0	7	0	HY	9	18	0
P03	HY	13	20	1	PR	3	14	0
P04	PR	15	35	0	HY	31	28	2
P05	HY	15	34	0	PR	9	18	0
P06	PR	3	13	0	HY	9	20	0
P09	HY	15	26	0	PR	11	13	1
P10	PR	7	8	1	HY	12	29	0
P11	HY	6	15	1	PR	2	8	0
P12	PR	9	15	0	HY	9	18	0
P13	HY	8	15	0	PR	2	17	0
P14	PR	7	17	0	HY	13	23	0
P15	HY	8	19	1	PR	6	23	0
P16	PR	5	11	0	HY	19	23	0
P18	PR	4	11	0	HY	25	38	1
P19	HY	10	31	0	PR	7	19	0
P21	PR	2	18	0	HY	22	35	0

Table 2: The total number of edits concerning conceptual and procedural encodings in MT and IMT conditions.

Text	MT CE	PE	Text	IMT CE	PE
PR/HY	131	299	HY/PR	193	348

total number of edits (*M*= 26.9 for MT and *M*= 33.8 for IMT, *t*(15) = 1.31, *ns*). Likewise, we found no difference in the number of CE edits contrasting MT to IMT (8.2 ≈ 12.1), neither in PE (18.7 ≈ 21.2). These results did not corroborate our first hypothesis.

As for one of our main objectives, we found a significant difference in the total number of edits between CE and PE in MT condition, 8.2 (CE) < 18.7 (PE), *t*(15) = -7.38, *p* < .01, as well as in IMT condition, 12.1 (CE) < 21.2 (PE), *t*(15) = -7.21, *p* < .00001. Thus, we can confirm our second hypothesis and that the results are in line with those in Alves & Gonçalves (2013) in the investigation of encodings in human translation, revealing that post-editing tasks are also mostly driven by instances of procedural encoding edits, whichever the condition is.

On the one hand, we have found a proportion of less than 30% of CE edits against more than 70% of PE edits in the MT condition. Furthermore, in the IMT condition we have found that CE edits corresponded to more than 30% of the total number of edits while PE edits accounted for a little less than 70% of the total number of edits, which indicates a higher proportion for PE against CE, as shown in Table 3.

Table 3: Reporting the total number of edits of CE and PE in each condition

	Texts mixed			
Conditions	MT (16)		IMT (16)	
Encodings	CE	PE	CE	PE
absolute	91	295	224	392
relative	24%	76%	36%	64%
t(15)	-7.38		-7.21	
	p < .01		*p* < .00001	

These results are in line with those by Alves & Gonçalves (2013), namely 42.5% of edits related to CE against 57.5% of edits related to PE in human translation with significant difference. Note that, in both PEd conditions, PE edits were significantly higher than CE edits. From this observation, PE is more edited than CE in PEd, even higher than in human translating, indicating that machine translation systems tend to be more productive when dealing with CE-related items (vocabulary and terminology) than with PE-related items (morph-syntax).

Having assessed the number of CE- and PE-related edits in MT and IMT conditions, our next step was to verify the cognitive effort spent on these post-editing tasks, thus, we present in the next session the analysis of eye tracking data.

4.1.2 Fixation count, fixation duration and the average of fixation duration

We tested the effect of MT and IMT conditions on variables such as fixation count and fixation duration and observed larger numbers in IMT condition in both fixation count and fixation duration, as shown in Figure 6. Using the Wilcoxon test, results show a statistically significant difference between these conditions [for all the participants, $V = 136$, $p < .05$ (1768.25 (IMT) > 901.56 (MT)].

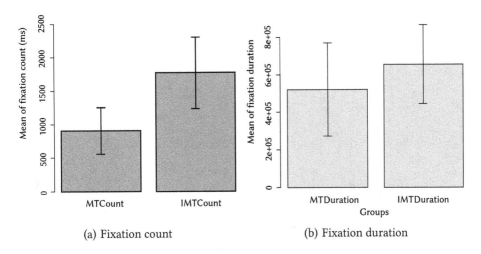

(a) Fixation count   (b) Fixation duration

Figure 6: Mean fixation count/duration for MT and IMT

Interestingly, when comparing average fixation duration (as it is demonstrated in Figure 7), the value in MT is greater than in IMT. We tested this difference and observed that the average fixation duration of MT is significantly longer than that in IMT [520684.13 (MT) < 653518.38 (IMT), $V = 0$, $p = 0.03$]. One may point out that the duration of fixations can vary according to the workbench system in use, consequently, the type of post-editing task. In this sense, we interpret that in terms of fixation data, fixation for reading translation options in IMT condition can be different from that related to processing translation from scratch, as well as that related to non-interactive post-editing, i.e., what may possibly include *from-scratch-type* of problem solving. Under this assumption, we checked the average and the median of MT and IMT fixation durations (Table 4). According to Lykke Jakobsen & Jensen (2008), data concerning to eye movements such as fixation count and fixation duration is sensitive depending on task where reading is predominantly involved. Thus, we find reasonable to postulate that in the IMT condition, fixation duration is more closely related to reading than to *from-scratch-type* of problem solving.

With regard to reading behaviour in IMT workbench, Table 4 presents interesting data. Despite the higher number of alternative possibilities and the relatively

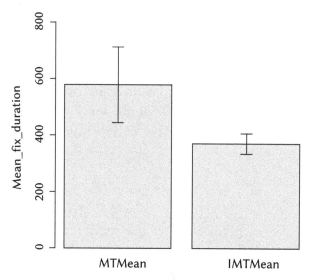

Figure 7: Average fixation duration in MT and IMT (in milliseconds)

greater number of CE edits performed in this condition, as mentioned earlier, the average fixation duration indicates the effectiveness of the interactive mode, since the effort spent on building up implicatures from the identified encoding problems seems to be reduced by these alternative possibilities offered by the system, generating a higher number of fixations with shorter fixations on average. This result may indicate that, in spite of the apparently higher processing effort in IMT condition, due to the higher fixation count and fixation duration observed, there was probably less cognitive effort in this condition. Introducing the median value, that is, the central value of a dataset, it can also characterize the participants' reading behaviour, buffering pushing up or down effects of some outliers. Recognizing that both the mean and median value in MT is much higher than in IMT, we argue that the median fixation duration in IMT reminds the mean fixation duration of reading text for comprehension presented by Just & Carpenter (1980), 225 ms, as well as presented by Rayner (1998), 200-300 ms. Even though we may need more sophisticated methodology to measure this difference, one of the reasons for this significant difference is that a delay in mean fixation duration probably is an indicator for the kind of cognitive activities involved, other than reading. Therefore, it requires some qualitative explanation about the fundamental difference between the two post-editing conditions, as we will discuss below.

This result coherently fits our theoretical framework, as RT assumes that building up explicatures and implicatures from scratch (human translation) or from

Table 4: The mean and median for fixation duration in MT and IMT conditions

	Mean	Median
MT (Total)	578.74	400
IMT (Total)	369.97	266

just one unsatisfactory option offered (MT condition) will be more effortful in terms of cognitive processing in translation than doing this assisted by some more options (IMT condition), as the initial process of articulating CE, PE and HE in the target language translation-unit is anticipated by the system. Therefore, results in Table 4 indicate that in MT condition, fixations can more probably be related to reading plus problem-solving processes, while in IMT condition they are much more related to reading and less to problem-solving processes.

4.1.3 Relating the encoding data and the eye tracking data

Finally, we calculate the average fixation duration per edit, that is, the average fixation duration divided by the average number of edits in each condition in order to observe the contributions that each condition offers. When comparing the two conditions, results present a larger average fixation duration for the MT condition (29 (MT) > 11 (IMT), $t(15)$ = -4.80, p < .001). Therefore, the fourth hypothesis was confirmed.

Table 5: Average fixation duration per edit by condition

(ms)	Total MT(16)	IMT(16)
Average per unit of edits	29	11
Results	$t(15)$ = -4.80	
	p < .001	

4.2 Discussion

4.2.1 Considerations about edits on encodings

Our results suggest that CE and PE-related edits, in both MT and IMT conditions, are in line with the results found by Alves & Gonçalves (2013), the first quantitative study to observe cognitive effort upon edits during human translation underpinned by Relevance Theory (Sperber and Wilson 1986/1995). Accordingly, our current research provides evidence that PE-related edits are still more prevalent than CE-related events in post-editing tasks. This not only corroborates the findings of Alves & Gonçalves (2013), but it also suggests that both MT and IMT conditions are mostly driven by instances of edits related to procedural encodings, which could mean that machine translation outputs seem to help solve more CE-related problems than PE-related ones.

In line with relevance-theoretic assumptions, this evidence also highlights the role of PE-related edits to constrain and control inferential processes in post-editing. Consequently, we confirm the validity of a relevance-theoretic approach to the analysis of post-editing. We claim that the analysis of the number of edits on three different categories, namely CE, PE and HE, is a promising way to characterize multilingual text production tasks such as translation and post-editing.

Concerning the difference between MT and IMT in terms of edits, the results did not present any significant difference. From these results, we understand that, even if the IMT workbench suggests options whenever the post-editor types one or two characters, the options appear somehow in a controlled manner for the post-editors to choose the best one among them. We may argue that two possible and concurrent factors could have caused this result: one is related to the participants' unfamiliarity with IMT post-editing; the other factor relates to the prediction accuracy of the IMT system.

In terms of unfamiliarity, Underwood et al. (2014: 553) mention that "post-editors' performance tended to increase as they became acquainted with the interactive system over an 18-month period". Therefore, as our participants were not used to do post-editing in the IMT condition, it seems that the facilitating effect expected to be generated by the interactive condition could not be fully observed in the experiment by means of a reduction in the number of edits and a reduction in the total task time. With regard to the total task time, according to Alves et al. (2015), in a study carried out with the same set of data, participants spent significantly more time when post-editing with interactivity, Wilcoxon signed-rank Test $z = 10$, $p = 0.001$, in other words, 1005161 milliseconds (16min 45s) on MT and 1225812 milliseconds (20min 25s) on IMT.

In terms of prediction accuracy of the IMT system, we could observe that, in spite of the lack of significant difference in the amount of edits between MT and IMT conditions, as well as the unexpected increase in the IMT condition total task time, a facilitating effect[1] of assisting the post-editor stemming from inter-active support could be observed. This finding corroborates the results of Sanchis-Trilles et al. (2014), in which the authors compare MT and IMT post-editing tasks in terms of total time required to produce the final translation and the amount of key strokes performed during the task. Their results show that, even with lit-tle training, IMT post-editing can be as productive as standard MT post-editing in terms of total time required to perform the task, as fewer keystrokes were required in the IMT task. Accordingly, our data also suggest that IMT can be as productive as MT in terms of encoding edits performed in both conditions, re-vealing that the "ready-to-insert" solutions offered by the IMT system demanded low-processing effort from the post-editors, as we discuss below.

4.2.2 Considerations about the eye tracking data

As O'Brien (2008) points out, interpreting eye tracking data is not a straightfor-ward task. Our results indicate greater fixation count and fixation duration in IMT post-editing than in MT post-editing. This difference can be interpreted in relation to the number of words automatically offered in the IMT condition: this increase is rather expected, as number of words increase along the task in the IMT. What has drawn our attention is the mean and median value of fixation du-ration: both values are greater in MT than in IMT tasks. As we have commented earlier, it may be related to a distinctive behaviour in post-editing. Lykke Jakob-sen & Jensen (2008) identified in their study about reading modalities that mean fixation duration is different, depending on the task type. The Danish partici-pants' mean fixation duration in reading an English text varied from 205 ms in reading for comprehension to 235 ms in sight translation. Their results confirm that, as far as (standard) human translation is concerned, fixation duration on the source text area is different from fixation duration on the target text area. Addi-tionally, there are also differences between translation students and professional translators in terms of cognitive processing. Building on their results, we postu-late that there must be typical reading patterns and different processing effort for MT post-editing and IMT post-editing. If a post-editor expects a type of op-tion to be offered by the IMT system and his/her expectations are met, this may influence his/her behaviour – with less fixation count and less fixation duration.

---

[1] We consider a facilitating effect here only as the main factor in the reduction of the amount of cognitive effort and time spent by the post-editor in the production of the target text's first version once it is given by the machine output. Therefore, it is not to be mistaken with semantic priming or schema activation effects observed in similar and closely implemented translation/post-editing experimental tasks.

If the IMT system, on the contrary, offers unexpected options against standard language conventions that human translators would be likely to render, this may result in an increase in fixation count and fixation duration.

Rayner (1998), when talking about the basic characteristics of eye movements in information processing, reports that mean fixation duration during silent reading is 225 ms, while mean fixation duration during typing is 400 ms. These fixation durations figures support the assumption that the IMT fixation duration is closely related to a reading process type, once we have found a similar pattern as IMT mean/median fixation duration was 369/266 ms, respectively, and MT mean/median fixation duration was 578/400 ms, respectively, both representing significant differences between MT and IMT.

Likewise, we assume that the MT mean fixation duration is closely related to a typing mean fixation duration, in which fixations are relatively longer, not only because of cognitive processes of encoding and inferring, but also because of the typing activity occurring more frequently in the MT post-editing task. Rayner (1998: 396) points out that longer fixations during typing are explained by the fact that "the eyes wait in place for the hand to catch up". Hvelplund (2015) argues that this could very well mean that the eyes focus for longer at the same area not because a particular difficult item is being processed but because the mechanical operation of typing is slower than reading.

CAT tools, such as MT or IMT systems, can be equipped with a variety of optional windows. O'Brien (2008) reports on the relation between fuzzy matches and eye tracking data with users of SDL TRADOS. She defined one of the AOIs set up in the fuzzy match rate area, which was not frequently visited by participants: the respective mean fixation count is 25.60, while other AOIs' mean fixation count varies from 79 to 1354. However, the average fixation duration (234.92 ms) on these AOIs is similar to those of other AOIs (between 215 – 255 ms). In this sense, our results concerning the fourth hypothesis make sense in terms of global analysis: the average fixation duration per edits demonstrate post-editors' greater effort in MT, fixating their eyes longer on fewer number of edits.

Drawing on relevance-theoretic assumptions, we can also argue that the prevalent number of PE edits over the number of CE edits is an indicator of cognitive effort geared to solving particular problems of a morph-syntactic nature, which often occur in post-editing tasks. Krings & Koby (2001) postulate that there are two types of cognitive effort required in post-editing. One is at a lower level, at which post-editors mainly seek linguistic correctness, while the other is at a higher level, involving the post-editor's engagement with the discourse level.

Oppositely, CE-related edits can be potentially unlimited when translators become more aware of the ST meaning, as CE belong to open lexical classes (Moeschler 1998). Due to the way it encodes content, CE provides information directly related to mental representations. According to Alves (2001), one tries to recover the conceptually encoded information conveyed by the sender's mental representations by means of inferential processes. As the MT condition is a traditional human post-editing task with no assistance other than the machine translation output itself, we believe that post-editors are relatively free to engage in CE-related editing by means of inferential processes, which may indicate a more active commitment in terms of building a coherent target text rather than merely implementing a linguistic correction. Expert post-editors, as far as the quality of machine output and the principle of post-editing are concerned, most likely preserve the MT output, adjusting the target text as it was constructed by MT system, rather than passing their own cultural and stylistic filter. In relevance-theoretic terms, the optimal post-editing tool is required to reduce inferential work in building the options to be considered in the establishment of the interpretative resemblance, not only linguistic correction.

5 Concluding remarks

In this paper, we have set about measuring and comparing eye movements referring to the number of edits on *conceptual and procedural encodings* (CE and PE) between two post-editing tasks, namely with and without interactive support (IMT and MT conditions respectively). The main objective was to compare these two modes in order to investigate cognitive effort through the observation of instances of encoding-related edits and the usability and impact of an IMT system in the execution of a post-editing task.

Four hypotheses were proposed:

Hypothesis 1 predicted that there would be a lower number of editing events in the IMT condition than in the MT; this first hypothesis was not corroborated by our data analyses. Two possible reasons for this result are the unfamiliarity of the participants with IMT post-editing tasks, and the prediction accuracy of the IMT benchmark itself. Nevertheless, since no significant difference between the interactive and non-interactive total task time was observed, one may conclude that the IMT condition, even with little training, can be as productive as the MT condition.

Hypothesis 2 postulated that instances of procedural encoding-related edits would be proportionally more prevalent than edits related to conceptual encodings when considering post-editing tasks; this second hypothesis was corroborated in the present study.

Hypothesis 3 predicted that the mean and median duration of an eye-fixation should be shorter in the IMT condition when compared to the MT; a fact observed in our data analyses. Moreover, we noticed that the values obtained in the IMT framework are closely related to the ones expected for reading tasks. This may indicate that participants in the IMT condition tend to perform edits more related to reading for checking and revising than for writing and editing, the latter being more frequent in the MT condition.

Finally, hypothesis 4 postulated that the average fixation duration per edit should be shorter in IMT than MT condition; this hypothesis was also confirmed by our data.

Based on the four hypotheses, our findings indicate that interactive and non-interactive machine translation involve two different types of cognitive processes, and the facilitating effect found in the interactive condition might be related to a reduction in cognitive processes related to encoding and inferring, but also related to a reduction in the mechanical operation of typing. In order to be able to make a more substantial claim, we need to carry out further studies to expand some of the discussions presented in this article and check the results from this study with a thorough description of post-editors' behaviour which is still unknown.

This may offer an opportunity to understand with greater accuracy the differences in terms of cognitive/processing effort in post-editing tasks carried out with and without interactivity. These shortcomings, notwithstanding, appear to contribute to research in the field of post-editing.

Appendix

Text 1

What Protaphane is and what it is used for

Protaphane is human insulin to treat diabetes. Protaphane is a long-acting insulin. This means that it will start to lower your blood sugar about 1½ hours after you take it, and the effect will last for approximately 24 hours. Protaphane is often given in combination with fast-acting insulin products.

If you are allergic hypersensitive to this insulin product, metacresol or any of the other ingredients (see 7 Further information).

What to do in an emergency for more about hypos.

Take special care with Protaphane

Using other medicines

Many medicines affect the way glucose works in your body and they may influence your insulin dose. Listed below are the most common medicines which may affect your insulin treatment. Talk to your 102 doctor or pharmacist if you take or have recently taken any other medicines, even those not prescribed.

Your need for insulin may change if you also take: oral antidiabetic products; monoamine oxidase inhibitors (MAOI)

Pregnancy and breast-feeding

If you are pregnant, planning a pregnancy or breast-feeding: please contact your doctor for advice.

Driving and using machines

If you drive or use tools or machines: watch out for signs of a hypo. Your ability to concentrate or to react will be less during a hypo. Never drive or use machinery if you feel a hypo coming on. Discuss with your doctor whether you can drive or use machines at all, if you have a lot of hypos or if you find it hard to recognise hypos.

Talk about your insulin needs with your doctor and diabetes nurse.

Text 2

The active substance in Hycamtin, topotecan, is an anticancer medicine that belongs to the group 'topoisomerase inhibitors'. It blocks an enzyme called topoisomerase I, which is involved in the division of DNA. When the enzyme is blocked, the DNA strands break. This prevents the cancer cells from dividing and they eventually die. Hycamtin also affects non-cancer cells, which causes side effects.

How has Hycamtin been studied?

Hycamtin as an infusion has been studied in more than 480 women with ovarian cancer who had failed one treatment with platinum-containing anticancer medicines. Three studies were 'open', meaning that the medicine was not compared to any other treatment and the patients knew that they were receiving Hycamtin. The fourth study involved 226 women, and compared Hycamtin with paclitaxel (another anticancer medicine). The main measure of effectiveness was the number of patients whose tumours responded to treatment. Hycamtin has also been studied in three main studies in 656 patients with relapsed small cell lung cancer. One study compared Hycamtin capsules with symptom control alone and another compared Hycamtin as an infusion with Cyclophosphamide, Doxorubicin and Vincristine (a standard combination of chemotherapy). The third study compared Hycamtin given as an infusion and as capsules. The effectiveness was measured by looking at survival or response rates. Hycamtin as an infusion has been studied in 293 women with advanced cervical cancer, where the effectiveness of a combination of Hycamtin and Cisplatin was compared with that of Cisplatin alone. The effectiveness was measured by looking at overall survival.

What benefit has Hycamtin shown during the studies?

In ovarian cancer, the studies showed the effectivenes s of Hycamtin, with an overall response rate of about 16%. In the main study, 21% of the patients who received Hycamtin (23 out of 112) responded to treatment, compared with 14% of the paclitaxel patients (16 out of 114). In lung cancer, looking at the results obtained in all three studies, the response rate was 20% (480 patients received Hycamtin).

References

Alabau, Vicent, Ragnar Bonk, Christian Buck, Michael Carl, Francisco Casacuberta, Mercedes García-Martínez, Jesús González, Luis Leiva, Bartolomé Mesalao, Daniel Ortiz, et al. 2013. Advanced computer aided translation with a web-based workbench. In *2nd Workshop on Post-Editing Technologies and Practice*, 55–62. Citeseer.

Alves, Fabio. 2001. *Teoria da relevância & tradução: Conceituações e aplicações.*

Alves, Fabio. 2007. Cognitive effort and contextual effect in translation: A relevance-theoretic approach. *Journal of Translation Studies* 10(1). 18–35.

Alves, Fabio, José Luiz Gonçalves & Karina Sarto Szpak. 2014. *Some thoughts about conceptual/procedural distinction in translation.* Vol. 6. Valencia, Spain: Universitat de Valencia.

Alves, Fabio & José Luiz Gonçalves. 2003. A relevance theory approach to the investigation of inferential processes in translation. *Benjamins Translation Library* 45. 3–24.

Alves, Fabio & José Luiz Gonçalves. 2007. Modelling translator's competence: Relevance and expertise under scrutiny. In Yves Gambier, Miriam Shlesinger & Radegundis Stolze (eds.), *Translation studies: Doubts and directions*, 41–58. Amsterdam/Philadelphia: John Benjamins.

Alves, Fabio & José Luiz Gonçalves. 2013. Investigating the conceptual-procedural distinction in the translation process: A relevance-theoretic analysis of micro and macro translation units. *Target* 25(1). 107–124.

Alves, Fabio & Daniel Vale. 2009. Probing the unit of translation in time: Aspects of the design and development of a web application for storing, annotating, and querying translation process data. *Across Languages and Cultures* 10(2). 251–273.

Alves, Fabio & Daniel Vale. 2011. On drafting and revision in translation: A Corpus Linguistics oriented analysis of translation process data. *Translation: Computation, Corpora, Cognition* 1(1). 105–122.

Alves, Fabio, Arlene Koglin, Bartolomé Mesa-Lao, Mercedes García Martínez, Norma B de Lima Fonseca, Arthur de Melo Sá, José Luiz Gonçalves, Karina Sarto Szpak, Kyoko Sekino & Marceli Aquino. 2015. Analysing the impact of interactive machine translation on post-editing effort. In Michael Carl, Srinivas Bangalore & Moritz Schaeffer (eds.), *New directions in empirical translation process research*, 77–94. Bern: Springer.

Alves, Fábio, José Luiz Gonçalves & Karina Szpak. 2012. Identifying instances of processing effort in translation through heat maps: An eye-tracking study using multiple input sources. In Pushpak Bhattacharya Michael Carl & Kamal Kumar Choudhary (eds.), *24th international Conference on Computational Linguistics*, 5–20. Mumbai: COLING.

Aziz, Wilker, Maarit Koponen & Lucia Specia. 2014. Sub-sentence level analysis of machine translation post-editing effort. In Sharon O'Brien, Laura Winther Balling, Michael Carl, Simard Michel & Lucia Specia (eds.), *Post-editing of machine translation: Processes and applications*, 170–199. Newcastle upon Tyne: Cambridge Scholars Publishing.

Barrachina, Sergio, Oliver Bender, Francisco Casacuberta, Jorge Civera, Elsa Cubel, Shahram Khadivi, Antonio Lagarda, Hermann Ney, Jesús Tomás, Enrique Vidal, et al. 2009. Statistical approaches to computer-assisted translation. *Computational Linguistics* 35(1). 3–28.

Blakemore, Diane. 2002. *Relevance and linguistic meaning: The semantics and pragmatics of discourse markers.* Cambridge: Cambridge University Press.

Carl, Michael, Barbara Dragsted, Jakob Elming, Daniel Hardt & Arnt L. Jakobsen. 2011. The process of post-editing: A pilot study. In *Proceedings of the 8th international NLPSC workshop*, 131–142. Frederiksberg: Samfundslitteratur.

Casacuberta, Francisco, Jorge Civera, Elsa Cubel, Antonio L Lagarda, Guy Lapalme, Elliott Macklovitch & Enrique Vidal. 2009. Human interaction for high-quality machine translation. *Communications of the ACM* 52(10). 135–138.

De Almeida, Giselle. 2013. *Translating the post-editor: An investigation of post-editing changes and correlations with professional experience across two Romance languages.* Dublin City University PhD thesis.

De Sousa, Sheila C. M., Wilker Aziz & Lucia Specia. 2011. Assessing the Post-Editing effort for automatic and semi-automatic translations of dvd subtitles. In *Recent advances in natural language processing (RANLP-2011)*, 97–103. Hissar, Bulgaria.

Depraetere, Ilse. 2010. What counts as useful advice in a university post-editing training context? Report on a case study. In *EAMT 2010: Proceedings of the 14th annual conference of the European association for machine translation.* Saint-Raphaël, France.

Federico, Marcello, Alessandro Cattelan & Marco Trombetti. 2012. Measuring user productivity in machine translation enhanced computer assisted translation. In *Proceedings of the Tenth Conference of the Association for Machine Translation in the Americas (AMTA).*

Fiederer, Rebecca & Sharon O'Brien. 2009. Quality and machine translation: A realistic objective. *The Journal of Specialised Translation* 11. 52–74.

Gonçalves, José Luiz. 2003. *O desenvolvimento da competência do tradutor: Investigando o processo através de um estudo exploratório-experimental.* 241 f. Tese (Doutorado 45 em Estudos Lingüísticos). Belo Horizonte, Brazil: Faculdade de Letras da Universidade Federal de Minas Gerais.

González-Rubio, Jesús & Francisco Casacuberta. 2014. Cost-sensitive active learning for computer-assisted translation. *Pattern Recognition Letters* 37. 124.

Green, Spence, Jeffrey Heer & Christopher D Manning. 2013. The efficacy of human post-editing for language translation. In *Proceedings of the SIGCHI conference on human factors in computing systems*, 439–448. ACM. Paris, France.

Guerberof Arenas, A. 2012. *Post-editing MT output/posedición de traducción automática.* Argentina: Colegio de Traductores Públicos de la Ciudad de Buenos

Aires. http://www.traductores.org.ar/nuevo_org/home/cursos_presenciales/
?id_ruta=6&nivel=526&nivel3=130&nivel4=131&id_curso=1020&mes=05%
ano=2010.

Gutt, Ernst-August. 1991. *Translation and relevance: Cognition and context.*
Manchester: St Jerome.

Just, Marcel A. & Patricia A. Carpenter. 1980. A theory of reading: From eye
fixations to comprehension. *Psychological Review* 87(4). 329.

Krings, Hans P. & Geoffrey S. Koby. 2001. *Repairing texts: Empirical investigations
of machine translation post-editing processes.* Vol. 5. Kent, Ohio: Kent State University Press.

Langlais, Philippe & Guy Lapalme. 2002. Trans type: Development-Evaluation
cycles to boost translator's productivity. *Machine Translation* 17(2). 77–98.

Loffler-Laurian, Anne-Marie. 1984. Machine translation: What type of post-
editing on what type of documents for what type of users. In *Proceedings of
the 10th international conference on Computational Linguistics*, 236–238. Association for Computational Linguistics. Stanford, CA, USA.

Loffler-Laurian, Anne-Marie. 1996. *La traduction automatique.* Villeneuve d'Ascq:
Presses Univ. Septentrion.

Lykke Jakobsen, Arnt & Kristian Tangsgaard Hvelplund Jensen. 2008. Eye movement behaviour across four different types of reading task. *Copenhagen Studies
in Language* 36(1). Susanne Göpferich, Arnt Lykke Jakobsen & Inger M Mees
(eds.). 103–124.

Mesa-Lao, Bartolomé. 2013. Eye-tracking post-editing behaviour in an interac-
tive translation prediction environment. In Kenneth Holmqvist, Fiona Mulvey
& Roger Johansson (eds.), *Book of abstracts: 17th European Conference on Eye
Movemement*, 541. Lund University.

Moeschler, Jacques. 1998. Directional inferences and the conceptual/procedural
encoding distinction. In *Proceedings ot the Relevance Theory Workshop*, 3–8.

O'Brien, Sharon. 2004. Machine translatability and post-editing effort: How do
they relate. In *Translating and the computer*, vol. 26.

O'Brien, Sharon. 2006. *Machine-translatability and post-editing effort: An empirical study using translog and choice network analysis.* Dublin, Ireland: Dublin
City University.

O'Brien, Sharon. 2008. Processing fuzzy matches in translation memory tools:
An eye-tracking analysis. *Copenhagen Studies in Language* 36(1). 79–102.

Ortiz-Martınez, Daniel, Germán Sanchis-Trilles, Francisco Casacuberta, Vicent
Alabau, Enrique Vidal, José-Miguel Benedı, Jesús González-Rubio, Alberto San-
chis & Jorge González. 2012. The CASMACAT project: The next generation

translator's workbench. In *Proceedings of the 7th Jornadas en Tecnologıa del Habla and the 3rd Iberian SLTech Workshop (IberSPEECH)*, 326–334.

Plitt, Mirko & François Masselot. 2010. A productivity test of statistical machine translation post-editing in a typical localization context. *Prague Bulletin of Mathematical Linguistics* 93. 7–16.

Pouliquen, Bruno, Christophe Mazenc & Aldo Iorio. 2011. Tapta: A user-driven translation system for patent documents based on domain-aware statistical machine translation. In *Proceedings of th 15th International Conference of the European Association for Machine Translation (EAMT)*, 5–12.

Rayner, Keith. 1998. Eye movements in reading and information processing: 20 years of research. *Psychological Bulletin* 124(3). 372–422.

Sanchis-Trilles, Germán, Vicent Alabau, Christian Buck, Michael Carl, Francisco Casacuberta, Mercedes García-Martínez, Ulrich Germann, Jesús González-Rubio, Robin L Hill, Philipp Koehn, et al. 2014. Interactive translation prediction versus conventional post-editing in practice: A study with the CasMaCat workbench. *Machine Translation* 28(3-4). 217–235.

Sjørup, Annette C. 2013. *Cognitive effort in metaphor translation: An eye-tracking and key-logging study*. Copenhagen, Denmark: Copenhagen Business School.

Skadiņš, Raivis, Maris Puriņš, Inguna Skadiņa & Andrejs Vasiļjevs. 2011. Evaluation of SMT in localization to under-resourced inflected. In Mikel L. Forcada, Heidi Depraetere, & Vincent Vandeghinste (eds.), *15th international Conference of the European Association for Machine Translation*, 35–40.

Somers, Harold L. 2001. Machine translation, applications. In M. Baker (ed.), *Routledge encyclopedia of translation studies*, 136–141. London, New York: Routledge.

Specia, Lucia. 2011. Exploiting objective annotations for measuring translation post-editing effort. In M. L. Forcada, H. Depraetere & V. Vandeghinste (eds.), *Proceedings of the 15th Conference of the European Association for Machine Translation*, 73–80.

Specia, Lucia, Marco Turchi, Nicola Cancedda, Marc Dymetman & Nello Cristianini. 2009. Estimating the sentence-level quality of machine translation systems. In *13th Conference of the European Association for Machine Translation*, 28–37.

Sperber, Dan & Deirdre Wilson. 1986. *Relevance: Communication and cognition*. Oxford: Blackwell (second edition 1995).

Underwood, Nancy L, Bartolomé Mesa-Lao, Mercedes García-Martínez, Michael Carl, Vicent Alabau, Jesús González-Rubio, Luis A Leiva, Germán Sanchis-Trilles, Daniel Ortíz-Martínez & Francisco Casacuberta. 2014. Evaluating the effects of interactivity in a post-editing workbench. In *LREC*, 553–559.

Wilson, Deirdre. 2011. The conceptual-procedural distinction: Past, present and future. In V. Escandell-Vidal, M. Leonetti & A. Ahern (eds.), *Procedural meaning: Problems and perspectives*, 3–31. Bingley: Emerald.

Wilson, Deirdre & Dan Sperber. 1993. Linguistic form and relevance. *Lingua* 90(1). 1–25.

Chapter 7

Eye tracking and beyond: The dos and don'ts of creating a contemporary usability lab

Christoph Rösener

Johannes Gutenberg University of Mainz/Germersheim

Many research facilities and institutions contemplate the idea of setting up an eye tracking laboratory or an even more extensive usability lab of their own. However, from the initial idea to the successful implementation of such a project, there are lots of difficulties and problems, which have to be solved. Everything from room size and layout, to which technology to use, which devices to purchase and the choice of software and the methods to be used (Dumas & Redish 1999) – there are many questions to answer during the conception and construction of such a laboratory. Despite this, eye tracking, as the major technique in usability research, has become more sophisticated and complex over recent years. Moreover, in usability laboratories additional equipment is needed, which in many cases has to interact with the eye tracking devices. All these are obstacles, which have to be overcome in the process of creating an eye tracking or usability laboratory. In the present paper, I will try to approach these issues from various points of view, showing the dos and don'ts in the process of setting up such a laboratory.

1 Introduction

In this paper I will try to approach the various challenging issues one faces in planning, designing and implementing a contemporary usability lab from various points of view, showing the dos and don'ts in the process of setting up such a laboratory. Following the introduction, I will give a brief overview of modern eye tracking equipment available on the market. Several eye tracking systems are presented as well as additional devices necessary for the task. Connected with this, I shall discuss some of the main issues important for the final decision regarding which system to choose. This is then followed by a description of possible design concepts for usability laboratories in general. Finally, I will describe

Christoph Rösener. 2016. Eye tracking and beyond: The dos and don'ts of creating a contemporary usability lab. In Silvia Hansen-Schirra & Sambor Grucza (eds.), *Eyetracking and Applied Linguistics*, 143–163. Berlin: Language Science Press. DOI:10.17169/langsci.b108.297

the difficulties and problems in using an eye tracking laboratory for usability studies. The paper ends with a presentation of the existing usability laboratory at Flensburg University of Applied Sciences and at the end some conclusions are drawn and future possibilities are discussed.

In order to get a common and clear understanding of what 'usability' means, it is first of all necessary to take a closer look on the various existing definitions. Standard 9241 from the International Organization for Standardization (ISO) defines 'usability' as "[t]he effectiveness, efficiency and satisfaction with which specified users achieve specified goals in particular environments." (International Organization for Standardization 2006). Effectiveness, efficiency and satisfaction are then further defined in the standard as follows:

> **effectiveness**: the accuracy and completeness with which specified users can achieve specified goals in particular environments

> **efficiency**: the resources expended in relation to the accuracy and completeness of goals achieved

> **satisfaction**: the comfort and acceptability of the work system to its users and other people affected by its use

In 1992, the multi-part standard was named "Ergonomic requirements for office work with visual display terminals". From 2006 on, the standards were retitled to the more generic "Ergonomics of Human System Interaction". Nevertheless, it is obvious that the focus of this definition is clearly only usability in connection with software applications. In 1998, Jakob Nielsen gave a wider definition of usability:

> Usability is the measure of the quality of the user experience when interacting with something -- whether a Web site, a traditional software application, or any other device the user can operate in some way or another.[1]

This definition includes, in addition to the classical software application, also 'any other device', i.e. to my mind also objects, tools or any other sort of device.

I will use this broader definition as a basis in order to develop the design of a contemporary usability lab. At the same time, I would like to point out that this definition expresses the wide range of possible research interests a contemporary usability lab can be used for. Concerning language and translation research, the

---

[1] Nielsen (1998); cited in Eichinger (1999).

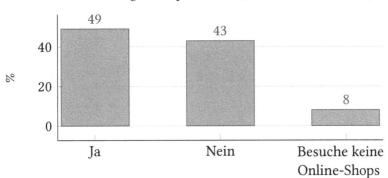

Figure 1: Usability of online shops (Source: TNS Emnid 2014).

most important method to investigate, for example, reading behaviour, comprehensibility of texts or translational behaviour is clearly eye tracking. Therefore, if only language and translation research are to be done, an eye tracking laboratory instead of a fully equipped usability laboratory might be sufficient.

1.1 Motivation

Figure 1 shows the results of a survey by the German TNS Emnid opinion in 2014. 1,000 individuals of over 14 years of age were asked the question "Have you ever left an online shop because the user interface was too difficult?". Possible answers were "yes", "no" or "I do not use online shops".

From the 92% of the web users who do use online shops, more than 50% consider web shops too complicated sometimes. That means that more than 50% of the web users are not satisfied with the quality and thus the usability of online shops. In contrast, in Figure 2 the results of a survey concerning the use of customer-oriented instruments for online retailers are shown. The participants were asked: "Which of the following customer-oriented instruments do you use or do you plan to use to improve the sales of your online shop?" The given list contained the following instruments:

- analyzing user behaviour to identify optimization potential

- customer surveys to identify improvement opportunities

- certification by a provider of quality seals

- usability evaluation by external vendors

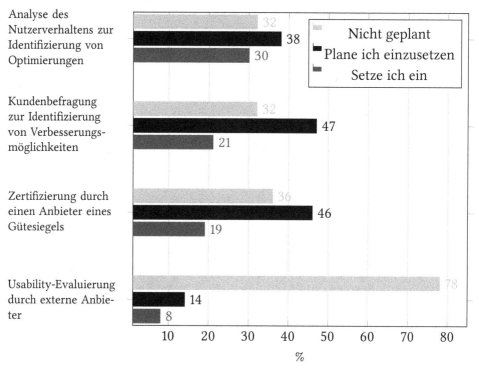

Figure 2: Instruments to improve the sales of online shops (Source: ibi research University Regensburg GmbH 2014)

Possible answers were "I use this", "I plan to use this" and "Not planned". The survey was conducted by ibi research University Regensburg GmbH.

The results show clearly that, despite the problem shown in Figure 1, very few online retailer actually use (8%) or plan to use (14%) usability engineering to improve their web sites. With these two statistics alone, the large potential of usability engineering and research becomes clear. These findings can therefore well serve as a motivation to design and create a contemporary usability lab.

1.2 Methods and techniques

To achieve the abovementioned goal "to measure the quality of the user experience", various research methods and techniques exist:

- observation

- pre- and post-test questionnaires

- (retrospective) interviews

- paper prototyping

- co-discovery learning, etc.

- think-aloud protocols

- keyboard and mouse logging

- video and audio recording, etc.

Furthermore, in addition to all the methods and techniques above, eye tracking is a key research method conducted in every usability laboratory. So, on the one hand a contemporary usability laboratory should provide the latest eye tracking equipment. On the other hand, all of the abovementioned methods and techniques for usability research should also be technically supported.

1.3 Starting point

At Flensburg University of Applied Sciences, eye tracking research was planned mainly in two scientific fields. One was eye tracking for language and translation research, i.e. research concerning reading behaviour, gaze pattern analysis and the comprehensibility of texts (Hennig & Tjarks-Sobhani 2007). The other field was eye tracking for usability engineering, i.e. to analyze, test and evaluate software interfaces (especially of language and translation software) (Hansen-Schirra & Rösener 2013), to test and evaluate online manuals and online help in technical communication (especially on mobile devices), to investigate operation of machinery (operating cycles, work processes), to analyze, test and evaluate web and software interfaces in other areas (for example, mechanical and electrical engineering). Furthermore, for future projects research concerning industrial design and design rationale respectively were envisioned.

It was thus very clear that eye tracking should serve two purposes in the future usability laboratory at Flensburg University of Applied Sciences: as a key research method for language and translation research as well as a key research method for usability testing. That meant that these two different approaches had to be implemented in the same laboratory. This in turn had a significant impact on the choice of which equipment and software systems to purchase and on the laboratory design.

2 Eye tracking and usability engineering

2.1 Eye tracking systems – spoilt for choice

The first problem to deal with when implementing a contemporary usability laboratory is the manifold variety of technical equipment, especially concerning the eye tracking equipment. Holmqvist states that "in 2009 we found 23 companies selling video based eye tracking systems" (Holmqvist et al. 2011: 12). In my view, however, there are only a small number of traditional manufacturers providing equipment for academic research[2]:

- ASL – Applied Science Laboratories, Bedford, USA

- SMI – Sensomotoric Instruments, Teltow, Deutschland

- SR-Research, EyeLink System, Ottawa, Kanada

- Tobii, Danderyd, Sweden

Of course, there are many more new competitors, like, for example, Mangold International GmbH, Arnstorf, Interactive Minds GmbH, Dresden, both Germany and Eyetech, Digital Systems, Mesa, USA to name but a few. However, these manufacturers in my opinion offer equipment more for media and advertisement consultants than for profound scientific research. Besides the manufacturer, the final buying decision should mainly be based on two questions: "What do I really need?" and "Which manufacturers meet my requirements?" The first decision that has to be taken is about which of the eye tracking working solutions are required for the planned laboratory. Basically, there are three different types of eye tracking systems: workstations, mobile solutions and eye tracking glasses. In Figure 3 an example of each solution is given.

As the name implies, mobile eye tracking solutions are designed for research in varying environments, for example, on-site research with laptops in companies. Eye tracking workstations on the other hand are laboratory-based and deliver the

---

[2] This selection is clearly subjective. However, it is definitely not the intention of the author to favour certain manufacturers. The selection is based on the author's experience and on discussions with colleagues working in other existing language and translation research eye tracking and/or usability laboratories. Thus, the list makes no claims of being complete.

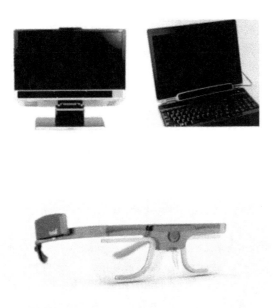

Figure 3: Eye tracking workstation, mobile eye tracker, eye-tracking glasses (Tobii 2014 / SMI 2014) Photographs CC-BY Tobii AB, CC-BY SMI

most accurate results. Finally, eye tracking glasses are suitable for fully mobile eye tracking studies, for example, operating machinery.

Additionally, there are a lot of properties to consider when purchasing an eye tracking system for a usability laboratory. At this point, I will briefly discuss only three main issues, which again in my view are very important for the final decision regarding which manufacturer to choose and which solution to buy: the sampling rate, the different solutions for testing mobile devices and the system license policy of each manufacturer. Other relevant parameters for comparison might be mobility, handling, workmanship, software features and of course price, to name but a few.

The decision to discuss only the three abovementioned issues was taken for the following reasons: The sampling rate is of major interest especially when planning to do language and translation research in the usability lab, because when investigating reading behaviour or comprehensibility of texts, for example, you have to deal with very rapid eye movements. The solutions for testing mobile devices are taken into account because more and more mobile devices, instead of stationary computers, are used for tasks like reading texts, editing texts and so on. From the point of language research, that makes this issue very important for the design of a future-oriented usability laboratory. And finally, the systems license policy is chosen as an issue because it is very difficult within public institutions like universities to achieve long term financing for projects or equipment. Therefore, the license terms and conditions of the manufacturers are of major importance to achieving a sustainable long term solution for the planned usability laboratory.

2.1.1 Sampling rate

As noted by Holmqvist et al. (2011: 29) "[t]he sampling frequency is one of the most highlighted properties of eye trackers by manufacturers, and there is a certain competition in having the fastest system." The sampling rate is measured in Hertz (Hz = times per second) and various systems with sampling rates from 25-30 Hz up to more than 1000 Hz do exist. Reasons for not purchasing a fast system can be that high-speed eye trackers are more expensive, that they are more restrictive to the participants and that they produce larger data files. On the other hand, a high sampling rate is necessary for certain eye tracking measures as shown in Figure 4.

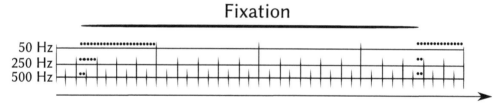

Figure 4: Fixation recorded at different sampling frequencies (Holmqvist et al. 2011: 31)

On top of Figure 4, you have a fixation of a certain time shown as solid line. Along the timeline of the figure, each small peg stands for a photo of the eye. Then the gaze position is calculated and a sample is recorded. The errors – indicated with dashed lines in the figure – are much larger for slower systems. Of course, there are also other eye tracker specific properties for data quality, for example, latency (saccadic latency, saccadic velocity and acceleration) as well as accuracy and precision. However, the decision which system to purchase depends first of all on the question of what you need to detect or measure. It can be stated that the faster the eye movement you want to analyse the faster your system and the sampling rate respectively has to be. For more information about the influence of the sampling rate on eye tracking research setup and results see Andersson (cf. Andersson, Holmqvist & Nyström 2009).

2.1.2 Testing mobile devices

As shown in Figure 5 different manufacturers offer various solutions for testing mobile devices.

Figure 5: Mobile device stands and eye tracking glasses (Tobii 2014; SMI 2014)
Photographs CC-BY Tobii AB, CC-BY SMI

For testing of mobile devices, so called mobile device stands (MDS) as well as eye tracking glasses are suitable. However, each solution has its advantages and disadvantages. Mobile device stands provide a very accurate analysis of small design elements, because the mobile device is always fixed in the stand and thus the data recording is of better quality. Eye tracking glasses will definitely not deliver the same data quality. On the other hand, the participant-device interaction is unnatural with mobile device stands. As illustrated in Figure 5, both MDS solutions fix the mobile device. Even worse, between the two rods of the MDS, shown on the right side in Figure 5, no movement of hands is possible, because as the eye tracker is mounted underneath the mobile device, any movement of the hands here would make eye tracking impossible.

On the other hand, eye tracking glasses can be used very flexibly. The glasses can be worn almost like ordinary glasses. Thus, a natural participant-device interaction is guaranteed, as you can use the glasses in day-to-day situations, for example, using a tablet computer in an armchair. As a result, a HD video of the field of view is recorded, with a point indicating where the participant looks. The only disadvantage of that setting might be that with the eye tracking glasses the analysis of small design elements is not of the same quality as with a MDS. Again the decision which solution to choose depends on the research preferences.

2.1.3 System license policy

Another last important point to consider when purchasing software for an eye tracking or usability laboratory is the system license policy of each manufacturer. Here significant differences do exist, which can be crucial for the final decision. Especially the following conditions have to be taken very carefully into account:

- purchase or rental

- support and updates

- upgrade cycles and method

- various software packages for different tasks

- network licenses (work with student groups)

The decision whether to buy or rent a software system is often influenced by the administration of the universities. Usually – especially within project funding – the universities prefer one-time instead of regular payments. Therefore, a rental solution is often out of question. In addition, the support and future updates should be included in the purchase. Some manufacturers offer only fee-based support and updates, which is again difficult to realize within projects. It is also very important to know, whether the offered support is gradual and, if yes, which support I will get with the planned purchase.

Finally, also the type of support (ticket system, etc.), office hours and response time should be considered, as well as the upgrade cycles and method. A complicated upgrade method can be annoying and very time consuming and should be avoided for that reason. To take a closer look on the software packages offered is also recommended. It is very important that the eye tracking software allows one to analyze collected data on different computers, so that it is possible to work with groups of students. Additionally, for a convenient research and teaching situation, it should be possible to run several software systems at the same time, so that analyzing data on several computers in a pc network with groups of students becomes possible.

2.2 Deploying a usability laboratory to serve all interests – the Swiss army knife

When deploying a usability laboratory, one of the most difficult tasks to fulfil is to serve the different interests of the future users of the laboratory. All the different research areas have to be taken into account, especially when a broad multidisciplinary use of the laboratory is planned. First of all, for eye tracking for language and translation research it is necessary that the eye tracking equipment operates at a high sampling rate. Only this enables research in the area of reading behaviour, gaze pattern analysis and comprehensibility of texts. To serve this research interest the purchase of an eye tracking workstation is mandatory.

On the other hand, usability engineering requires mobile solutions for eye tracking. Here a high sampling rate is not as important as the mobile aspect. Usability research should be possible not only in the laboratory but also in natural participant-device interaction in day-to-day situations outside the usability lab. Therefore, mobile eye tracking solutions as well as eye tracking glasses are needed. Only with this equipment is it possible to do, for example, on-site research of operation of machinery and web and software interfaces.

Additionally, usability engineering requires further equipment of the laboratory as well. For example, video cameras and microphones, several video screens and special usability software to process the collected data (e.g. 'Morae' from TechSmith) are necessary to conduct research not only in the area of software interfaces and human computer interaction, but especially in the area of industrial design and design rationale. The main focus in this field is user observation, interviews and think aloud protocols. To conduct this kind of research video and audio equipment as well as special user experience and market research software is needed. Moreover, when it is planned to combine results from electroencephalography (EEG) recordings with the usability testing, the laboratory needs to be equipped with a brain computer interface or EEG system respectively. And of course, all software systems should work together, i.e. have common interfaces so that recorded data can be exchanged without any problems.

The same applies to experimental design and setup. If research is planned and conducted in all the abovementioned fields, the laboratory should be suitable for all possible different experimental designs and setups, which means there should be enough space for equipment, participants and test objects in the laboratory. To fulfill these requirements at least two rooms – one laboratory (test room) and one observation room, separated by a wall with a one way mirror – are necessary. Figure 6 shows a possible layout of a usability laboratory.

Of course, several layouts for usability laboratories are possible. For example, the 'executive observation lounge' in Figure 6 is not essential for running a successful usability laboratory. It might be interesting though for a third group of observers to discuss the test without disturbing the experimenters and usability specialists in the observation room (cf. Nielsen 1993: 203ff.). In my view for academic purposes, the one laboratory solution is absolutely sufficient. Naturally, if larger groups or a lot of participants should be tested simultaneously a multi-laboratory solution would be appropriate. However, this applies rather for bigger companies, where series of tests with large groups are conducted.

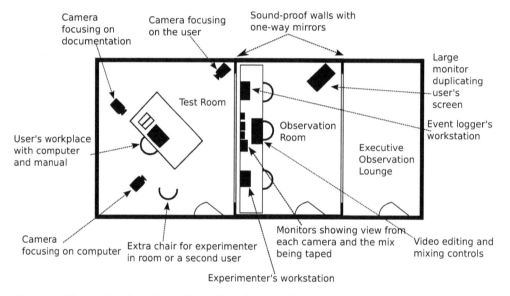

Figure 6: Floor plan for a hypothetical usability laboratory (adapted from Nielsen 1993: 201)

In addition to the room or space problem, there are many other necessary properties of the recording environment, which have to be considered when developing a contemporary usability laboratory. It would be far too much to list all possible circumstances, which can cause problems for the experimental setup or lower the quality of the data recorded in the usability lab. Nevertheless, I want to point out a few conditions, which are important in my opinion and easy to consider in order to avoid problems before or during usability tests. Cramped recording space, for example, makes it uncomfortable for the participants to attend usability experiments. Therefore, you have to make sure that the participants themselves feel comfortable before and during the actual usability tests. One precondition to achieve this is enough room space. The lab should be spacious enough so that the participants do not feel cramped. Lab availability correlates with that. If the lab is only available in very restricted times, it becomes very difficult to get the participants to show up. Regular working hours of the usability laboratory help to counter this problem.

Sunlight in the laboratory is another problem. It can affect eye tracking experiments by creating optic artifacts and imprecision. Of course, you can dim the laboratory with sun blinds, but the best solution for a usability laboratory is to have either windows to the north, so that sunlight never shines into the lab, or no windows at all, at least in the test room. Another problem connected with this is lamps and lighting conditions in general. Depending on how and which lamps are positioned under the ceiling in relation to the eye tracking equipment this might also cause imprecision as well as optic artifacts. The best solution is to use neon light instead of light bulbs or halogen lamps, and to create lighting conditions in the usability laboratory, which can be changed manually, for example, with dimmer controlled lamps and electrically adjustable shades.

It is also advisable to minimize various sources of electromagnetic noise. In order to avoid inaccuracy, low precision or – in the worst case – data loss try to locate your usability laboratory away from lifts and ban fans and other electronic equipment causing electromagnetic noise from your usability lab as well as from the neighbouring rooms. The same applies for vibrations and noise. Try to avoid people moving nearby as well as noise and vibrations caused by outside traffic. This can seriously affect your data quality. It is therefore advisable to use a soundproof room. However, this is often impossible for financial reasons.

2.3 The dos and don'ts – the most common mistakes

Concerning the dos and don'ts in the process of developing and implementing a contemporary usability laboratory there are – in my view – two main areas of most common mistakes: theoretical mistakes and practical mistakes. The most common theoretical mistakes to mention, when starting to develop the idea of a usability laboratory, are mistakes concerning the imagination of experiment design and experimental setup. Most of the time, the future users of a usability laboratory have a very good idea of what they want to test or analyze. But they have not thought about what exactly they want to know or investigate. To take one example, the idea is to test the comprehensibility and the usage of machine operating manuals. But what exactly should the test scenario be and what kind of results should test which assumption is not clear at all.

In a lot of these cases the eye tracking or usability equipment is purchased before the experiment design and the experimental setup is well conceived. Quite often future users have not thought about what kind of results they want to achieve, when the order for the equipment is placed. And because of this, after a while, it becomes clear that certain equipment, additional software or other pre-conditions, which would be necessary to conduct specific experiments, have not been foreseen or ordered in the process of the implementation of the laboratory. This can lead to a significant level of frustration and – even worse – to the situation that a brand new usability laboratory is then no longer used by the initially very interested user groups, because their expectations could not be fulfilled. Do not expect especially the experimental setup to be easy. It is worthwhile to sit together with all interested future user groups and discuss and develop a detailed plan, what kind of experimental setup each different user plans to realize in the lab, before you start the implementation of the new usability laboratory and be-fore you order the equipment and software systems respectively.

The most common practical mistakes happen when the usability laboratory is already implemented and running. Quite often, the optimistic expectations of the new users are very soon disappointed when they start their first experiments in the new lab. Out of the manifold difficulties, which may occur, once you get started with usability experiments, I would like to point out a few general prob-lems here, which can cause immediate frustration and disappointment. A big problem, for example, are eye tracking experiments with wearers of glasses or contact lenses. This is something new users should be absolutely aware of. It is very difficult, if not impossible, to conduct experiments and/or to get high quality eye tracking data from experiments with wearers of glasses or contact lenses. This is particularly interesting because the manufacturers are quite re-served about this fact and talk rather hesitantly, if at all, about it. Definitely, in experiments with wearers of glasses or contact lenses more problems than ex-pected will occur. Some of the manufacturers encounter this problem providing corrective lenses at least for the eye tracking glasses. Nevertheless, the problem persists with stationary and mobile eye trackers.

Another point is the adjustment or configuration of the system. At the begin-ning, quite often users do not pay much attention to the adjustment or configura-tion of the eye tracking equipment and the software respectively. And then they are disappointed when the results they get are not of very good quality. Here again, it is worthwhile to spend some time with an initial training how to adjust and configure the system. The better the configuration and the adjustment of the system, the better the quality of the data finally recorded.

Despite these two main points, there are a lot of other factors which influence the quality of the recorded eye tracking data. For example, the fact that all participants are different concerning nose size, head form, distance between the eyes, etc. requires a very careful experimental setup. Some of the manufacturers try to encounter several of these problems by providing, for example, different types of nose rests, adjustable glasses and special software possibilities. However, that helps only to a certain extent. The common practical mistake is too little time spent to do the setup of the system very carefully. The same applies for the furniture of the actual test or observation room. An important point here is the types of chairs for the participants. Make sure that no swivel chairs are used. These chairs make the participants move more than necessary and thus cause bad data quality. For the same reason the chairs should not have adjustable armrests nor adjustable back or seating surfaces. All this causes bad data quality or even loss of data. The table for the eye tracking workstation is another sensitive point. Due to the various heights of the participants, the monitor and the eye tracker have to be adjusted each time in its horizontal position to fit the respective person. To prevent damage to the monitor and the eye tracker respectively because of this frequent adjustment, it is recommended to use an electrically controlled height-adjustable table instead. It is comfortable to use and damage to the eye tracking equipment or the monitor can be easily avoided. However, the most common mistake when developing and implementing a new usability laboratory is that the expectations of the users are often pitched far too high. Quite often too much is expected from the technology alone.

2.4 The usability laboratory at Flensburg University of Applied Sciences – an attempt

At Flensburg University of Applied Sciences, the new usability laboratory consists of two rooms. The observation room/control room size is about 11 m² and the actual test room/usability recording studio size is about 23 m². The rooms are separated by a wall with an inbuilt one way mirror. The floor plan/layout of the actual usability laboratory is shown in Figure 7.

There are two video cameras in the laboratory. The cameras are mounted under the ceiling in opposite corners of the test room/recording studio. Together with additional microphones, it is possible to record both audio and video data from the test room. Focused on the user and on the computer screen or documentation the cameras provide two video views, which can be mixed together with special software in the observation room/control room.

The usability laboratory at Flensburg University of Applied Sciences is an example for a compromise between an eye tracking laboratory for language and translation research only on the one hand and a fully equipped usability lab on the other hand. It combines features and possibilities of both worlds so that it serves most of the interests of the different future user groups.

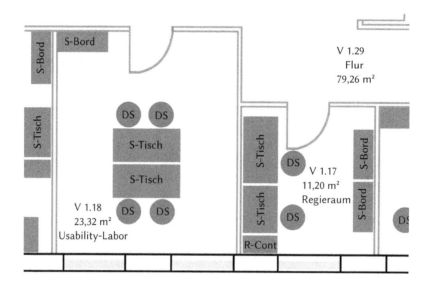

Figure 7: Floor plan / layout of the usability laboratory of Flensburg University of Applied Sciences (test room and small control room; separating wall with one way mirror)

3 Conclusion and outlook

Looking back at the process of planning, creating and implementing a contemporary usability laboratory at Flensburg University of Applied Sciences, I want to draw some key conclusions on the whole effort as well as to give some prospects about the desired possible future activities. The idea of developing a usability laboratory at Flensburg University of Applied Sciences came about two years ago. Based on an interdisciplinary cooperation between three courses of study, the course of study International Technical Communication, the course of study Applied Computer Science and the course of study Media Informatics, an initiative was launched to make an application to the Ministry of Education of Schleswig-Holstein for funding a human computer interaction and usability laboratory. When the funding was finally granted, a group of people started to work out a development plan and a roadmap for the two laboratories.

From the beginning, the plan was to use the usability laboratory not only within one single study course. On the contrary, it was clear from the start that the future usability laboratory has to provide research opportunities for usability engineering in general and eye tracking research in particular. Therefore, the persons involved in the development of the future usability laboratory were truly aware of the necessity to purchase not only eye tracking equipment. Nevertheless it was, even at this stage, difficult to meet all the requirements of the various interested user groups. Besides the so called 'language people', who were interested in language and translation research (reading behaviour, gaze pattern analysis and comprehensibility of texts, etc.), there were a lot of other people with different research interests: people from the department of economics, who wanted to do market research; people from the department of education of Flensburg University, who wanted to do gaze pattern analysis in picture reception; people from the department of mechanical engineering, who wanted to do research concerning the operating of machinery and so on and so forth. It soon became very clear that it was extremely difficult do meet all the existing demands of the different parties involved.

To solve this problem, the next step in planning the new usability laboratory was to collect the various ideas and research interests of the different future user groups and departments and transfer them into realistic experiment setup and experimental design respectively. This turned out to be very difficult as well. First of all, it was very difficult to really identify the demand of some interest groups. Some of the parties involved had only a very vague imagination about what they really wanted to do. Most of the time the problem was that they were not or only to some extent familiar with the subject of usability engineering or eye tracking research in general. So, already at this point, it is really necessary in the process that the people involved have some knowledge about the different techniques and methods used in usability engineering.

The second problem was to transfer the existing demands into real experimental design and setup. This requires also, even at this stage of the process, detailed knowledge about the possibilities of the different equipment and systems. Of course, this applies only for a smaller group of people, who are finally involved in placing the order for the equipment and software systems respectively. But it is nevertheless very important that these people have detailed knowledge about the potential and possibilities of various equipment and software systems.

At this point, I would like to mention another very interesting fact about the manufacturers of eye tracking equipment and systems. During the process of creating and implementing the usability laboratory at Flensburg University of

Applied Sciences, we had the experience that some manufacturers are very accommodating when it comes to discounts for universities. Some manufactures offer significant discounts for eye tracking equipment and software systems. The offers quite often come in the form of bundle software and hardware packages or as 'educational licenses', etc. Analyzing the sales policy of the relevant manufacturers can really save a lot of money in this context.

3.1 Recommendations

From the 'lessons learnt' point of view I would like to make some recommendations on the basis of which – in my view – a lot of problems can be avoided when implementing a contemporary usability laboratory, which should serve – in the best possible way – all research interests of the different parties and interest groups. It is extremely important to involve all possible future user groups in the planning already from the beginning. So, the first step in the process of developing a usability laboratory has to be the analysis of the situation at your university or institution. Ask the different parties and possible future user groups what kind of research they want to conduct in the planned laboratory. On this basis then clear experimental setups and designs should be developed. All this should be done before ordering the equipment, because it is very difficult, time consuming and annoying to cancel or change orders once they are placed. It is definitely much better to know what equipment and system is suitable to meet your special requirements. 'One step at a time' is the best strategy when planning and implementing a usability laboratory.

For the implementation and operation of a contemporary usability laboratory also keep in mind that technology is only as good as the people who use it. So again, from the beginning when you plan your resources you have to make sure that you have the staff to operate the laboratory in a proper way. Do not expect too much from the technology alone. A usability laboratory can not be operated without the appropriate staff. The administration and management of the laboratory when working with participants or whole user groups as well as the handling of the equipment and software systems require qualified and competent personnel. Moreover, in some cases it might even be necessary to have personnel to programme additional software to run certain experiments or analyse recorded data. Furthermore, if you intend to provide regular laboratory opening hours, appropriate staff will also be required.

3.2 Outlook

A sustainable implementation of any contemporary usability laboratory at a university or similar institution is – in my opinion – only possible if a few key principles are observed. These principles are multiplicity, integration, expertise and self determined learning. Multiplicity in this case simply means that the usability laboratory should be used by many different users and groups, for example, various courses of study from different departments and faculties. Thereby a high acceptance and recognition of the subject usability is ensured. Integration on the other hand guarantees for permanent utilization of the laboratory. If usability engineering becomes a proper component of teaching and research activities of several courses of study, the laboratory will be permanently in use. In addition, growing usability engineering expertise due to many interdisciplinary projects will lead to a more effective usage of the laboratory, and subsequently also to better (project) results.

Finally, student projects, based on self-determined learning principles and with the usability laboratory involved in the research, create a very attractive field of studies. Once the students start to develop their own research projects and conduct their own eye tracking or usability tests in the laboratory, usability engineering is well established as an attractive field of research in the courses of study. This could then, due to project papers and bachelor and master theses, lead to more "usability driven" contacts with companies and manufacturers on the market. And this in turn guarantees that the courses of study offered at the university are vocationally orientated and of high practical relevance. All the abovementioned points apply especially for Flensburg University of Applied Science. The full integration of the new usability laboratory into teaching and research activities of the university is the main objective and the desirable future for this laboratory.

References

Andersson, Richard, Kenneth Holmqvist & Marcus Nyström. 2009. Sampling frequency and eye-tracking measures: How speed affects durations, latencies, and more. *Journal of Eye Movement Research* 3(3). 1–12.

Dumas, Joseph S. & Janice Redish. 1999. *A practical guide to usability testing*. Bristol, UK: Intellect Books.

Eichinger, Armin. 1999. Usability. http://pc1521.psychologie.uni-regensburg.de/student2001/Skripten/Zimmer/usability.html, accessed 2016-07-18.

Hansen-Schirra, Silvia & Christoph Rösener. 2013. Proactive use of eye-tracking in the translational workflow. In Sambor Grucza, Monika Płużyczka & Justyna Zając (eds.), *Translation studies and Eye-Tracking analysis*, 139–152. New York: Peter Lang.

Hennig, Jörg & Marita Tjarks-Sobhani (eds.). 2007. *Usability und Technische Dokumentation*. Lübeck, Germany: Schmidt-Römhild.

Holmqvist, Kenneth, Marcus Nyström, Richard Andersson, Richard Dewhurst, Halszka Jarodzka & Joost Van de Weijer. 2011. *Eye tracking: A comprehensive guide to methods and measures*. Oxford: Oxford University Press.

International Organization for Standardization. 2006. *Ergonomics of human system interaction*. Geneva, Switzerland: ISO.

Nielsen, Jakob. 1993. *Usability engineering*. Amsterdam: Elsevier.

Nielsen, Jakob. 1998. The increasing conservatism of web users. http://www.useit.com/alertbox/980322.html, accessed 2016-07-01.

SMI. 2014. Sensomotoric instrument GmbH. http://www.smivision.com/en.html, accessed 2014-09-22.

Tobii. 2014. Tobii is the world leader in eye tracking. http://www.tobii.com, accessed 2014-09-22.

Chapter 8

The impact of nominalisations on the reading process: A case-study using the Freiburg Legalese Reading Corpus

Sascha Wolfer

Institute for the German Language, Mannheim

I present a study using eye-tracking-while-reading data from participants reading German jurisdictional texts. I am particularly interested in nominalisations. It can be shown that nominalisations are read significantly longer than other nouns and that this effect is quite strong. Furthermore, the results suggest that nouns are read faster in reformulated texts. In the reformulations, nominalisations were transformed into verbal structures. Reformulations did not lead to increased processing times of verbal constructions but reformulated texts were read faster overall. Where appropriate, results are compared to a previous study of Hansen et al. (2006) using the same texts but other methodology and statistical analysis.

1 Introduction

In linguistics, text corpora are used to analyse rules and usage of language in natural contexts. Most of the time, corpora are annotated with linguistic information. These annotations allow linguists to search for recurring patterns and extract all instances of a specific linguistic structure from the corpus. These linguistic annotations can span several levels of linguistic structures (e.g. parts-of-speech and phrase structure). On the textual level, one might be interested in co-reference chains to investigate which words in the text refer to the same entity in the world. Some annotations can also be numerical in nature. One of the most common measures associated with words is the frequency with which the word occurs in natural language. Most of the time, a corpus itself is the source of this information. If one compiles a corpus of terminological language, however, the frequency of words in everyday language might also be interesting. Here, the source of the frequency information might well be another corpus.

Sascha Wolfer. 2016. The impact of nominalisations on the reading process: A case-study using the Freiburg Legalese Reading Corpus. In Silvia Hansen-Schirra & Sambor Grucza (eds.), *Eyetracking and Applied Linguistics*, 163–186. Berlin: Language Science Press. DOI:10.17169/langsci.b108.298

Sascha Wolfer

In recent years, some researchers began to enrich corpora with another kind of annotation layer. If I collect or compile texts to create a corpus of natural language, I can take this corpus and show its contents to humans. Of course, these humans should be taken from a population likely to be confronted with the kind of text material I included in the corpus. The humans, who were exposed to my collected text material, are my readers. And while they are reading the text material, I can record their eye movements with an eye-tracker. In psycholinguistics, this method has been used for quite some time now. However, up until the last ten years or so, only carefully manipulated experimental stimuli were shown to readers. In psycholinguistic experiments, sentences might be constructed from scratch and only a single word could be exchanged for another to realise an experimental manipulation. Then, the effect of the experimental variation on processing behaviour is measured in form of reading variables (see §2.2 for a short introduction of reading variables).

If I record eye movements on natural text (i.e. the corpus I constructed), I can add those eye movements as an additional annotation layer. Now, a specific word is not only associated with a certain frequency measure, part-of-speech information and the phrase it is located in. It now also has processing information associated with it. With such a "reading corpus", I have a powerful instrument at hand to investigate human reading of natural texts. The linguistic information can still be used to select specific instances from the corpus, but now I also know how humans processed these instances when they read them in the context of the whole corpus. Collection of eye-tracking data is expensive (in terms of scientific staff, participants and time). That is the reason why reading corpora are a lot smaller than text corpora we are used to in linguistics.

Several reading corpora are available in the field of psycholinguistics. Most of them are in English (Frank et al. 2013; Kennedy 2003), but there are also reading corpora for French (Kennedy 2003) and German (Kliegl et al. 2004; Wolfer et al. 2013). In this article, I present analyses based on the Freiburg Legalese Reading Corpus (FLRC), a corpus of jurisdictional terminological language. Jurisdictional language is known (at least in Germany) for its difficulties on several linguistic levels. Hansen-Schirra & Neumann (2004: 170) following Oksaar (1988) and Wagner (1981) identify the following linguistic properties as representative for jurisdictional language: long sentences, personalisations of inanimate objects or circumstances, complexity induced by derivations (the creation of new words with affixes), chains of subordinated nouns, extensive genitive attribution, archaic forms, formulaic expressions and nominalisations instead of verbs. I will focus on the last-mentioned structures: nominalisations. The overarching research questions will be: Are nominalisations really harder to process than other words (especially than nouns, which are most comparable)? And can nominalisations be reformulated effectively to make text processing less complex?

I will start out by presenting some arguments why jurisdictional language should also be understandable to lay people (§1.1). I will then describe some reading corpora in more detail (§1.2). Chapter 2 will introduce the Freiburg Legalese Reading Corpus and the linguistic information (§2.1) and eye-tracking data it contains (§2.2). In Chapter 3, I will present my data selection and preparation processes (§3.1), formulate the hypotheses (§3.2) and present the statistical analyses and results (§3.3). I will discuss these results in Chapter 4. Chapter 5 will conclude the article.

1.1 Optimising the comprehensibility of jurisdictional language

The linguistic inaccessibility of jurisdictional language stands in contrast to the highly relevant function the jurisdictional system fulfils in modern democracies. Jurisdictional texts of all kinds ensure peaceful coexistence in our society. In Germany, the Bundesverfassungsgericht (Federal Constitutional Court) plays a prominent role in the German jurisdictional system and in society as a whole. On a linguistic level, its decisions are highly complex and not easily understandable for their ultimate addressees, the citizens of Germany who are mainly lay people when it comes to interpreting jurisdictional texts (cf. Eichhoff-Cyrus, Antos & Schulz 2009). Because of this prominent role of the Bundesverfassungsgericht, excerpts from decisions by this court were included into the reading corpus I am going to describe in this article. The corpus also contains full-length decisions. However, this part of the corpus will be of secondary interest in the present article.

Of course, one could say that jurisdictional language does not have to be understandable to lay people because it is a language for special purposes or professional jargon just like the language of, for example, IT staff, miners or linguists. Towfigh (2009) formulates such a position. There are (at least) two arguments against such a position. The professional jargons of IT people, miners or linguists are by far not as socially relevant as jurisdictional language. Of course, information technology also gets more important in modern social life. But still, it is far from being as important for the organisation of our social coexistence as jurisdictional language. If IT jargon might eventually get equally important, also the terminology of IT experts would face the demand of the public to get more understandable to everyone.

The second argument against the position that Towfigh (2009), amongst others, formulates is that even experts of the jurisdictional system struggle with their own professional code (cf. Eichhoff-Cyrus & Strobel 2009). As expected, 70% of all 84 surveyed legal experts judge their professional code as "weniger gut verständlich" (not well comprehensible) for lay people. Another 26% judge it as "nicht verständlich" (not comprehensible at all) for lay people (Eichhoff-Cyrus & Strobel 2009: 138). More surprisingly, though, 73% of the legal experts have *sometimes* trouble comprehending jurisdictional language themselves. Another 12% state that they *often* have trouble understanding jurisdictional language (Eichhoff-Cyrus & Strobel 2009: 146). The experts also largely agree that jurisdictional texts should be comprehensible for lay people without special training. Only 6% of all experts do not agree to this statement (Eichhoff-Cyrus & Strobel 2009: 139).

So, the demand for easier comprehensible jurisdictional language is formulated both by lay people and legal experts. With this motivation in mind, the Freiburg Legalese Reading Corpus was compiled. The goal was to provide detailed empirical data on the comprehension process of jurisdictional language. In terms of internal/external validity, some compromises were made in the Freiburg Legalese Reading Corpus: The part of the corpus with reformulations is clearly more similar to a classic psycholinguistic experiment because excerpts from original court decisions were reformulated by linguists making at least the reformulations not ecologically valid anymore. The other part of the corpus contains complete texts that were not altered. So, this part of the corpus can be considered ecologically more valid.

With this empirical data, hypotheses regarding the processing of specific linguistic constructions can be tested. Linguistic stimuli were not constructed from scratch but real-life linguistic stimuli were used, the aim being to reach high ecological validity. Hopefully, insights gained from these analyses can thus be generalised to other real-life texts.

1.2 Reading corpora

As already outlined in the introduction, research using reading corpora has gained increasing influence in psycholinguistics and related disciplines. Reading corpora are large collections of eye-tracking data on text material. There are already several reading corpora available in the field: The English UCL Corpus (Frank et al. 2013) contains eye-tracking and self-paced reading data. The German Potsdam Sentence Corpus (PSC, Kliegl, Nuthmann & Engbert 2006) consists of artificial sentences constructed around target words. These target words were selected for word class (noun or verb), frequency (high or low) and length (short, medium or long). For each of the 12 combinations of these factors, 12 sentences were constructed, leading to a total of 144 sentences. Please keep in mind that these sentences never occurred in the real world and are not connected to each other on a content level. The English/French Dundee Corpus (Kennedy 2003) contains editorials from *The Independent* and *Le Monde*. Recently, the PopSci corpus with German popular science texts has been introduced to the field (Müller-Feldmeth, Wolfer & Konieczny 2013). Here, 16 texts from popular science journals are contained in the text corpus and were read by human readers. So, connections between sentences on a textual level (e.g. co-reference chains) were still intact.

One of the first applications of reading corpora has been the evaluation of models of eye-movement control. There is still a considerable debate in this field, mainly between two models, the E-Z Reader (Reichle, Rayner & Pollatsek 2003) and the SWIFT (Engbert et al. 2005) model. Fairly low-level processes are the focus of both computational models. The models are mainly interested in when and where a reader moves the eyes while reading text. These low-level processes have to be considered, of course, but are not the primary focus of this chapter. Recently, higher-level processes in language comprehension have come to the attention of researchers using reading corpora. Several psycholinguistic models and theories have been investigated and evaluated using reading corpora: surprisal (Demberg & Keller 2008; Patil, Vasishth & Kliegl 2009), cue-based parsing and similarity-based interference (Müller-Feldmeth, Wolfer & Konieczny 2013), semantic constraint (Pynte, New & Kennedy 2008) and many more. In this article, I am going to investigate research questions dealing with the lexical level. Namely, I am going to analyse the processing of nominalisations and how, if at all, they can be reformulated.

2 The Freiburg Legalese Reading Corpus

All data for the Freiburg Legalese Reading Corpus was collected in the eye-tracking labs of the Centre for Cognitive Science at the University of Freiburg.

2.1 Language material

The Freiburg Legalese Reading Corpus consists of two main parts: (1) A subcorpus with nine original full length texts (three decisions, three press releases, and three newspaper articles) and (2) a sub-corpus containing thirty short sections of original decisions with thirty moderately reformulated texts and thirty

Table 1: Corpus design of the corpus part with the original excerpts and reformulations. Total token counts of the 10 texts in each cell are also shown. Column names are the three complexity types Hansen et al. (2006) used to select the original excerpts.

	Nominalisations	Complex NPs	Syntax
Original excerpts	10 texts	10 texts	10 texts
	200 tokens	303 tokens	434 tokens
Moderate reformulations	10 texts	10 texts	10 texts
	214 tokens	317 tokens	439 tokens
Strong reformulations	10 texts	10 texts	10 texts
	217 tokens	334 tokens	440 tokens

strongly reformulated texts. The first part consisting of full-length texts has 12,769 tokens. The second part with excerpts from decisions and the associated reformulations has 2,898 tokens. In the analyses, I will use data from both corpus parts but will focus on the second part (excerpts and reformulations) later on.

The excerpts and reformulations are especially useful for the analysis at hand. See Table 1 for a brief overview over the design of this corpus part. The thirty original excerpts were selected to meet one of three types of linguistic complexity (henceforth "complexity type"). Ten texts contain many nominalisations that were transformed into verbal structures during the course of reformulation (complexity type "nominalisations"). Ten texts contain very complex noun phrases – mostly due to excessive pre- or post-nominal modification (complexity type "complex NPs"). In the first reformulation step, these modifications were transformed into subordinate clauses. In the second step leading to the strongly reformulated version, sentences were split to avoid the sentential complexity induced by these subordinate sentences. The remaining ten original texts contained very long and multiply embedded sentences (complexity type "syntax"). They were split up repeatedly to achieve the moderately and strongly reformulated versions. All texts, including the reformulated versions, were taken from a study of Hansen et al. (2006). They reformulated the texts with the help of a jurisdictional expert who made sure that semantic content of the texts was maintained. Annotations of the texts were added by two student assistant annotators with the help of the software "Annotate" (Plaehn 1998) for semi-automatic syntactic annotation.

Parts-of-speech according to the Stuttgart-Tübingen-TagSet[1] and phrase structure were annotated. "Annotate" makes suggestions for both and the annotators
altered these annotations in case they were incorrect. When the annotators did
not agree on a certain annotation, agreement was established through discussion.
Nominalisations were identified manually.

Example 1 shows an original excerpt from the complexity type "nominalisations" (1a) and the associated strongly reformulated text (1b)[2]. From Example
1a, the original excerpt, in transition to Example 1b, the strong reformulation,
Hansen et al. (2006) transformed four *ung-nominalisations (*Herstellung, Redu-
zierung, Aufhebung, Aufhebung*) into verbal structures (*hergestellt wurde, redu-
ziert/aufgehoben wird, aufzuheben*).

(1) Mehr als zwölf Jahre nach der Herstellung der   deutschen
     More than twelve years after the realisation the.GEN German.GEN
     Einheit   habe   sich die Ermächtigung zur Reduzierung oder
     unity.GEN have.SBJV itself the authorization to reduction   or
     Aufhebung der   Gebührenermäßigung durch   Rechtsverordnung
     abolishment the.GEN reduction.of.fees   through legal.decree
     zu einer Rechtspflicht zur   Aufhebung des
     to a   legal.duty   for.the abolishment the.GEN
     Gebührenabschlags   verdichtet.
     partial.payment.of.fees condensed.
     'More than twelve years after the realisation of German reunification, the
     authorization for reduction or abolishment of a rebate of fees by decree is
     said to have been condensed to a legal duty of abolishment of rebates.'

(2) Mehr als zwölf Jahre nachdem die deutsche Einheit hergestellt wurde,
     More than twelve years after   the German unity   realised   was,
     habe   sich die Ermächtigung, dass die Gebührenermäßigung
     have.SBJV itself the authorization, that the reduction.of.fees
     durch   Rechtsverordnung reduziert oder aufgehoben wird,   zu der
     through legal.decree   reduced or   abolished is.AUX, to the

Rechtspflicht verdichtet, den Gebührenabschlag   aufzuheben.
legal.duty   condensed the partial.payment.of.fees abolish.

'More than twelve years after German reunification was realised, the authorization to reduce or abolish a rebate by decree is said to have been condensed to a legal duty of abolishing rebates.'

As already mentioned above, this does not change the semantic content of the text. Example 1 is a prototypical example in terms of reformulations of nominalisations. The frequently used nominalisations are transformed into verbal structures. However, as can also be seen in Example 1, subordinating structures have to be introduced to integrate these newly introduced verbal structures in the sentence context. These subordinating structures can be identified by the subordinating conjunctions *nachdem* and *dass* in Example 1b. Only nouns ending with -*ung* are treated as nominalisations in the remainder of this article.

When I analyse all 30 texts within the complexity type nominalisations (first column in Table 1), I see that the share of nominalisations in all words drops significantly from 16.8 % (originals) to 10.6 % (moderate reformulations) and 10.5 % (strong reformulations). Raw numbers for all 10 texts in each cell taken together are 35 (originals), 23 (moderate reformulations) and 23 (strong reformulations) nominalisations. So, obviously, no nominalisations were reformulated during the second step of the reformulation process[3]. To measure the impact of reformulations on the use of verbal structures, I sum up all occurrences of verbs and participles and look at the development of shares and raw figures over the reformulation versions. The verbal structures follow the opposite pattern of nominalisations. The share of verbal structures in all words rises significantly from 9.7 % (originals) to 20.0 % (moderate reformulations) and 21.1 % (strong reformulations). Again, most of the reformulations were obviously made between the originals and the moderate reformulations. The raw figures confirm this. The original texts contain 18, the moderately reformulated texts 41 and the strongly reformulated versions 45 verbs and/or participles. In the remainder of this chapter, I will investigate which influences these reformulations have on the reading process.

2.2 Eye-tracking data

All texts were distributed on pages that matched a 20-inch-flatscreen with a resolution of 1600 by 1200 pixels. Texts were presented in a 48 pt proportional serif

---

[3] For some of the texts, Hansen et al. (2006) did not create a strongly reformulated version.

font to allow for as natural as possible a reading experience. A maximum of 11 lines of text with 1.5 line spacing fit on one screen page. After each text, a comprehension question had to be answered by pressing 'yes' or 'no' on a response box. Questions were rather easy and were primarily included into the study to keep participants attentive. I used an SR Research EyeLink 1000 for data collection. The eye-tracker measured gaze position of the participants with a rate of 1000 Hz which produces 1 data point every millisecond. Calibration and validation was carried out before the experiment and – if necessary – data collection was interrupted to recalibrate the eye-tracker.

Reading data was collected from 80 human readers (40 for each corpus part) who were given course credit or monetary compensation for their participation. Participants were all students at the University of Freiburg with normal (56 participants) or corrected vision (24 participants). Data on the age of participants was not gathered. It was made sure that none of the participants had an educational background in law. 51 participants were female. Participants were seated with their heads on a chin rest, so that their eyes were approximately 60 cm away from the screen.

Reading time variables were calculated with custom R (R Core Team 2014) scripts from the fixation data collected and pre-calculated by the eye-tracker's data export tool (SR Research DataViewer). For the identification of fixations, I used the default parameter settings of DataViewer. Each fixation was associated to an interest area. Interest areas spanned individual words and were expanded vertically to the middle of the space between lines. Fixations not associated with an interest area were discarded.

The following reading variables can be considered standard measures in psycholinguistic reading research and were pre-computed for all words in the corpus: first fixation duration (the duration in milliseconds of the first fixation on the current word), first-pass reading times (the summed duration of all fixations from entering the word until exiting the word to the left or to the right), regression path durations (the summed duration of all fixations from entering the word until a word right of the word is fixated, including all fixations on material left of the word, i.e. regressions) and total reading times (the summed duration of all fixations on the word, also including fixations after the word has been exited to the right for the first time, i.e. if the reader re-reads the word later on). Several more reading variables can be calculated from these measures. For example, re-reading time (total reading time minus first-pass reading time) or a binary variable if a regressive saccade has been launched during the first reading of a word (is the regression path duration longer than the first-pass reading time?). Another variable that is frequently used is skipping probability that is derived from a binary variable if a word is read during first pass (is the first-pass reading time greater than zero?). Considering the whole FLRC, mean first fixation duration was 200 msec. Mean first-pass reading time was 265 msec. Mean regression path durations were 495 msec. Mean total reading times were 405 msec. On average, a regressive saccade was launched on 12.6% of all words in the FLRC.

I will not go into much detail regarding the cognitive processes associated with each of these reading time variables. This has been excellently done elsewhere in much more detail (Clifton, Staub & Rayner 2007; Hyönä, Lorch & Rinck 2003; Rayner & Pollatsek 2006). A few words have to be said, though. First-pass reading times include all fixations during reading a region of interest (here, regions of interest are words) for the first time. First-pass reading times therefore capture processes of word recognition and early stages of word processing. Regression path duration or go-past time, as it is also called, "can reasonably be construed as the time it takes upon reading the target word on first pass until it is successfully integrated with the ongoing context" (Rayner & Pollatsek 2006: 620). This, however, should not be the main problem of processing nominalisations. Of course, nominalisations have to be integrated into the context of the sentence – just as any other noun. However, I expect that the specific problem of processing a nominalisation has to do with derivation, and not with integration into the previous sentence context. So, I expect effects of nominalisations in rather early measures (e.g. first-pass reading time) and not in regression path durations. If I indeed find an effect in regression path durations and the probability of launching a regressive saccade upon encountering a nominalisation, this may be a hint that nominalisations are indeed harder to integrate into the previous context than normal nouns. An effect in total reading times cannot be ruled out because nominalisation may also be revisited after first pass.

3 The impact of nominalisations on the reading process

Nominalisations can be considered complex for two reasons. Hansen et al. (2006) describe them as an instrument to increase the informational density in a text: "Information is packed into heavy noun phrases and nominalisations rather than being distributed onto larger grammatical units [...]" (ibd., p. 24). Also, nominalisations can be used to create constructions like "die Abschiebung wird durchgeführt" (the deportation is carried out). Such constructions enable objective and pertinent descriptions ("objektive und sachbezogene Darstellung", Hansen-Schirra & Neumann 2004: 169) without mentioning a specific agent of the action. This may be odd for lay people and may lead to comprehension difficulties because such agent-less constructions are not very common in every-day language but rather have to be considered a property often found in terminological language (cf. Hansen-Schirra & Neumann 2004: 170).

Given the previously introduced linguistic material and the corresponding processing data, I am able to investigate several questions. The most obvious question is: Is it difficult to process nominalisations? This, however, is not a valid research question because no linguistic entity is mentioned to which nominalisations are compared. I will start by comparing nominalisations to all other nouns. I will then also compare the size of the effect nominalisations have on the reading process with the effects of other word classes (content/function words, finite verbs, all nouns). With this comparison, I want to estimate the relative size of the effect that nominalisations have on the reading process.

I will then go into detail using the part of the reading corpus that contains excerpts and reformulations. Ten texts were specifically selected because they contain many nominalisations. Those texts were reformulated in two steps. I will therefore check if the reformulations generally slow down the processing of verbs and participles. The final questions will be if overall text processing benefits from the reformulations of nominalisations. All research questions are also summarised in the first column of Table 2.

3.1 Data selection and preparation

Each research question posed above needs a specific subset of the reading corpus to be answered. The data subsets associated with the respective research questions can be found in the second column of Table 2.

After the respective data subset has been selected from the reading corpus, I have to control for some effects that are rather obvious but not interesting for the research questions at hand. For example, it is common sense that longer words take longer to read. Also, it has been shown repeatedly that corpus frequency is a good predictor for reading times. The more frequent the actual word (hitherto: word n) is encountered in natural language, the faster it is read (cf. Kliegl et al. 2004). This frequency effect extends to bigram and trigram frequencies, the corpus frequency of word n in combination with words $n - 1$ and, for trigrams, $n - 2$ (cf. Boston et al. 2008). Another factor that plays a crucial role for reading times is orthographic familiarity. Orthographic familiarity is a measure of how often a specific word shape appears in the language (cf. White 2008). Orthographic familiarity is operationalised by the cumulative frequency of all words with the same initial three letters and the same length as the critical word.

Table 2: Research questions, selected data subsets, and hypotheses for the analyses presented in this chapter

Research question	Data subset	Hypothesis
Are nominalisations harder to process than normal nouns?	All nouns (including nominalisations) in the FLRC	Nominalisations are read longer during first-pass.
How pronounced is the nominalisation effect compared to other classes of words?	All words in the FLRC	Compared to other word classes, the nominalisation effect is rather large.
Are nouns read faster after nominalisations have been reformulated?	All nouns in complexity type nominalisations	Nouns are read faster after nominalisations have been transferred to verbal structures.
Do reformulations shift complexity to verbal structures?	Verbs and participles in complexity type nominalisations	No observable effect
Does overall text processing benefit from the reformulations?	Whole texts of complexity type nominalisations	Reformulated texts are processed faster than original excerpts.

On the syntactic level, the position of word n in the sentence and its depth of embedding in the phrase structure are relevant predictors for reading times (cf. Pynte, New & Kennedy 2008). Words that occur later in the sentence are read faster. The same holds for words that are embedded deeper in the syntactic structure.

Other factors that can influence the reading times of words are related to the presentation of the words on the screen. The position of the text on the screen is relevant because, generally speaking, words appearing "later" on the screen are read faster. Also, reading behaviour on first and last words in lines can deviate from standard reading behaviour within a line. This is especially true for the first word in a row because it is the first word that is encountered after a change of text lines. If a reader changes the line, she or he has to initiate a very long saccade from the end of the line to the beginning of the next line. The fixation following this long saccade tends to be longer.

I control for all these factors by including the relevant variables word length, unigram, bigram and trigram frequencies, orthographic familiarity, position in the sentence, depth of embedding and presentation factors in statistical baseline models[4]. Participant and text identity were included as random intercepts into the models. When I analyse the effect of nominalisation, for example, the effect of the word's frequency is controlled for beforehand. This is desirable because, on the one hand, it reduces noise in my data and could lead to more pronounced effects of the factors I am interested in. On the other hand, this procedure also makes sure that variance in reading times that is really explained by word frequency or another control factor is not erroneously ascribed to other effects. Intuitively, the procedure leads to "cleaner" data and more reliable models.

3.2 Hypotheses

All hypotheses can also be seen in the third column of Table 2. If nominalisations are indeed more complex than normal nouns, I expect elevated first-pass (and eventually total) reading times for nominalisations compared to normal nouns. I would not necessarily expect an effect in regression path durations because the main problem of nominalisations should be a lexical one and not to integrate the nominalisations into the sentence context. At least, this should not be more of a problem than for normal nouns. When I compare the effect of nominalisations to the effects of other word classes, I would expect that the nominalisation effect is rather large. One could say that, the larger the nominalisation effect is in comparison to other effects, the more important it is to reformulate nominalisations or not to introduce them into texts in the first place. I will evaluate these first two hypotheses in the first section of the results section.

Regarding the reformulations, I would expect nouns to be read faster after nominalisations have been reformulated. This should simply be the case because the share of nominalisations in all nouns gets lower in reformulated texts (see §2.1 for statistics on the linguistic consequences of reformulations). The effect should be observable for first-pass (and eventually) total reading times.

I would also expect – if the reformulations were successful – that complexity is not simply shifted to another linguistic level or towards other linguistic

---

[4] The statistical baseline models are quite extensive and can be requested from the author. All models in the current article were fitted using linear mixed-effects models within the statistical environment R (R Core Team 2014) and the package lme4 (Bates et al. 2014).

structures, namely verbs and participles (see §2.1 for the relationship between reformulations and verbs and participles). If reformulations do not slow down processing of verbal structures, I do not expect an effect of reformulations on the reading times of verbs and participles. I will evaluate the latter three hypotheses in the second section of the results section.

For the last research question, I move away from the level of single words and take the whole texts of the complexity type nominalisations into account. This is a rather coarse grained measure that cannot tell us anything about the processing of single words. However, I can investigate the overall time it needs to process the original and reformulated texts as a whole. If reformulations were successful also on the textual level, I would expect slightly reduced reading times for the whole text for the reformulated versions.

3.3 Results

In this section, the research questions and associated hypotheses are categorised into two groups. The first group of research questions relates to the complexity of nominalisations in the whole reading corpus and the comparison to other word classes. The second group of research questions deals with the consequences it has on text processing when nominalisations are reformulated.

3.3.1 Complexity of nominalisations

For the first research questions, all nouns in the reading corpus were selected. Each of those nouns is associated with the information if it is a nominalisation or not. This is the only predictor I include into my model as a fixed effect. I calculated linear mixed-effects models for the reading time variables first-pass reading time, total reading time and regression path durations. Those reading time variables were corrected by the baseline model procedure introduced in §3.1 For skipping probability and the probability that a regressive saccade is launched upon encountering the noun, logistic mixed regression models were calculated. These models are better suited for binary outcome variables (cf. Jaeger 2008).

3 shows the model parameters for this first analysis. First-pass reading times, total reading times and also regression path durations are significantly higher for nouns that are nominalisations than for normal nouns. Please bear in mind that the effects for the reading time variables cannot simply be ascribed to word length (nominalisations are likely to be longer than normal nouns) because the baseline modelling rules this out beforehand. The probability of being skipped is significantly lower for nominalisations. The probability that a regressive saccade

Table 3: Model parameters (estimate, standard error and t value) for the fixed effect of a noun being a nominalisation. The five models for the different reading variables are in rows. P values are only available for the logistic mixed regression models for skipping probability and the probability of a regressive saccade (last two rows). For all other models, an absolute t value above 2 strongly indicates significance. The sign of the estimate indicates the effect direction.

	Estimate	Standard Error	t/z value
First-pass reading times	0.063	0.012	5.243
Total reading times	0.131	0.015	8.911
Regression path durations	0.073	0.020	3.615
Probability of being skipped	-0.536	0.033	-16.087
			$p < .0001$
Probability that a regressive saccade is launched	0.059	0.035	1.662
			$p = 0.10$

is launched upon encountering a nominalisation is *not* significantly higher than for normal nouns. This is somewhat surprising because the regression path durations are significantly higher for nominalisations. A likely explanation would be that first-pass reading times are also included in regression path durations and that the effect in regression path durations are really ascribable to the effect in first-pass reading times. So, I can conclude that nominalisations do not trigger more regressions back into previous text material than normal nouns. This relates to the question if nominalisations may also be harder to integrate into the sentence context than normal nouns. Given the results in Table 3, this does not seem to be the case. Nevertheless, the impact of nominalisations on context integration processes needs to be further investigated to tease apart these effects.

With the next analysis, I am comparing the nominalisation effect to other sets of words. I will concentrate on total reading times here, because the most pronounced effect was shown for this variable (second row of Table 3). I am going to compare the effect estimates because this model parameter can be thought of as an operationalisation of the effect strength[5]. I include all words in the reading corpus into this analysis. For each word, I code if it belongs to one or more of the following set of words: content words, function words, finite verbs, nouns, nominalisations. I chose finite verbs as a set for comparison because finite verbs

---

[5] In simple linear regression with only one predictor variable, the estimate is the slope of the regression line.

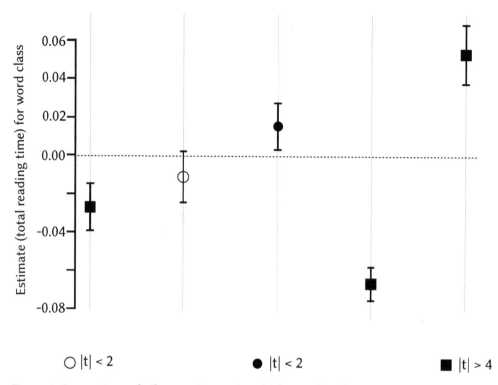

Figure 1: Comparison of effects estimates (y axis) for total reading times and the effects of being a content word, function word, finite verb, noun or nominalisation. The associated t value is symbolized by the plot symbols.

most of the time encode the main action going on in a sentence and should be considered quite relevant. With this coding, it is clear that each nominalisation belongs not only to the set of nominalisations but are also a subset of content words and nouns.

All those declarations that are either TRUE or FALSE for each word then enter one linear mixed-effects model as fixed effects. By comparing the estimates for the fixed effects, I get an impression of the relative importance of these estimates. The estimates are visualised in Figure 1. We are especially interested in the right-most point, the effect estimate for nominalisations. The estimate (β = 0.053, t = 6.80) is relatively high compared to all other effect estimates. This means that total reading times on a word are much higher when it is a nominalisation. This is surprising when I compare this estimate with the one for all nouns. The relatively low estimate (β = -0.066, t = -15.15) for nouns means that, if a word is a noun, total reading times on this word are much lower than for all other words. It can also be seen that the effect for nominalisations seems to be way stronger than the one for finite verbs (β = 0.016, t = 2.55) which have to be considered quite important elements in sentences.

3.3.2 Consequences of reformulating nominalisations

The results for the analyses of reformulations do not seem to be as clear as the ones introduced in the last chapter. If the reading times for the baseline models are used, no significant effects can be shown. All differences go into the right direction here (nouns are read faster in reformulated versions) but there seems to be too little explanatory power in the data to show significant effects here. If only word length, word frequency, word familiarity and presentation factors are included (see §3.1 for an explanation of these variables), a significant effect of reformulation can be shown. Since most of the reformulation is going on between the original excerpts and the moderately reformulated versions, both moderately and strongly reformulated versions are treated as "reformulated". This way, I only have the contrast between nouns in original and nouns in re-formulated texts. This makes the model parameters interpretable more easily. The model shows that nouns in reformulated texts are indeed read faster. This time, I only find a significant effect for first-pass reading times (β = -0.076, t = -2.05) but not for total reading times (β = -0.080, t = -1.22). The next question is if processing complexity shifts to verbs and participles when nominalisations are reformulated. For this analysis, I selected all verbs and participles[6] from the texts of complexity type "nominalisations". Verbs and participles were selected because nominalisations were transformed into verbal structures (see Example 1). It would be unfortunate for reformulation efforts if processing complexity simply shifts to the "substitute structures" that are introduced when nominali-sations are reformulated (also see Table 2). No effects can be shown for either first-pass reading times (β = -0.011, t = -0.20) or total reading times (β = -0.106, t = -1.65) and all effect estimates point into the negative direction, i.e. verbs and participles are read slightly (and not significantly) *faster*. Please note, if no effect can be shown, this does not mean that there really is no effect. It could always be the case that I simply cannot *detect* the effect. However, if reformulations re-ally would lead to increased reading times on verbs and participles because these were the structures that were introduced by transforming nominalisations, then the reading times in the reformulated version should be *higher*, which is not the case.

---

[6] In the tag set I used, verbs and participles are all words from one of the following parts-of-speech: VAFIN, VMFIN, VVINF, VVFIN, VVIZU, VAINF, VVPP, VMPP, VAPP.

To answer the last question, I take the analyses to the text level and compare the reading times of the different reformulation versions of the texts from the complexity type nominalisations. Indeed, as Table 4 shows, the mean reading time per text is getting lower as texts are reformulated. However, the noise (standard deviations, second column) is also very high here. Apart from that, I also have to take text length into account, because it is not that big of a surprise that texts are read faster if they are shorter. Indeed, they get a little shorter in average as the third column of Table 4 shows.   To tease apart the effect of text

Table 4: Mean text reading times, standard deviations and mean text lengths for texts with complexity type nominalisations

	Mean text reading time	Standard deviation	Mean text length
Original excerpts	9489 ms	7607 ms	149 characters
Moderate reformulations	8487 ms	7748 ms	144 characters
Strong reformulations	8018 ms	6193 ms	143 characters

length and relate the noise to the effect, I have to calculate a statistical model. Reformulation version and text length (as a control factor) are entered as fixed effects and participants and text identity are treated as random intercepts. I predict the logarithm of text reading time[7]. As expected, there is a clear effect of text length on text reading time ($\beta = 0.006$, $t = 5.16$), texts are read longer when they contain more characters. Apart from that, the effect I am interested in is also significant and it points into the direction the hypothesis suggests. Strongly reformulated texts are read faster than the original excerpts ($\beta = -0.157$, $t = -2.58$). Moderately reformulated texts, however, lie somewhere in between the originals and the strong reformulations ($\beta = -0.109$, $t = -1.79$) and are not significantly different from either one of them in terms of text reading time. Again, this does not replicate the findings of Hansen et al. (2006). There are several possible reasons for this: (1) I used a different method to measure text reading time. I summed all total reading times of all words. Hansen et al. (2006) measured the time between text presentation on-set till participants advanced to the question. (2) Hansen et al. did not correct for text length when estimating reading times. (3) Also, to my knowledge, they did not include random intercepts for participants and/or text

---

[7] The effects I report are even more pronounced when raw text reading time is predicted. However, it is statistically more appropriate to predict logarithmized text reading times because they follow a normal distribution more closely than raw text reading times.

identity. That means that inter-individual differences (between texts and/or participants) are not accounted for. (4) Hansen and colleagues analyse reading time differences over all complexity types while I only analysed texts of the complexity type "nominalisations" because these are the texts relevant for the current research question.

4 Discussion

All hypotheses mentioned in the third column of Table 2 were confirmed by the statistical analyses. Indeed, nouns, which are nominalisations, are read slower. This is confirmed by significant effects for first-pass reading times and total reading times. Also, nominalisations are less likely to be skipped. Although nouns in general are read faster than all other words in the reading corpus, this effect is the other way around for nominalisations. The effect size for nominalisation (i.e. the impact on the reading process) is comparable and even higher than the same effect for finite verbs.

So, nominalisations really seem to be quite complex for the reader to process. However, I also showed that – at least in my reformulation corpus – they can be reformulated. In the reformulated versions of the original excerpts, nominalisations were transformed into verbal structures. When comparing the reading times of nouns in the original versions with those in the reformulated versions, I found significantly faster reading on all nouns. It also does not seem to be some kind of trade-off where I just switch complexity introduced by nominalisations for complexity on verbs and participles. Those did not seem to be read longer in reformulated text versions. When using the very rough measure of overall text reading time, I saw that reformulated texts are read slightly faster. So, although nominalisations indeed seem to introduce a fair bit of complexity into jurisdictional texts, they obviously can be reformulated without just shifting processing complexity to another linguistic level.

However, I still have to bring these results into line with the larger context of text processing and text comprehension. It has been shown during the course of this article that nominalisations take longer to process and this is a quite pronounced effect. However, I did not present any data on the consequences for the mental representation the participants built up while reading the texts. Such consequences could be measured by asking participants to answer questions after reading the texts. This also has been done during data collection for the FLRC. I used the same questions like Hansen et al. (2006). However, the questions did not seem to be sensitive enough to measure improvements (or declines) in comprehension performance. Questions after all versions of the texts were answered similarly well. 84% of all questions after original excerpts were answered correctly, which is already a quite good result. For reformulated versions, this figure only rose marginally to 88% for moderately reformulated texts and 87% correctly answered questions for strongly reformulated texts. This does not replicate the results of Hansen et al. (2006) who found overall significantly better results for the moderate reformulations (approximately[8] 85% correct answers) than for the original excerpts (75%) and the strongly reformulated versions (78%). I do not have a clear explanation for these differences.

Note, however, that Hansen et al. only report overall results, i.e. the other complexity types with complex noun phrases and complex syntax are also included in their analysis. As a consequence, it is not possible to compare my results concerning only the complexity type "nominalisations" with the results of Hansen et al. (2006).

5 Conclusion

Jurisdictional texts are complex on many linguistic levels. One of the main difficulties is a large amount of nominalisations. Indeed, those seem to be associated with slower comprehension processes. Fortunately, I also showed that this complexity could be resolved by transforming the nominalisations into verbal structures. However, more research is necessary to also investigate the consequences for the mental representations readers construct in their minds while reading jurisdictional texts. Just because some parts of the texts are read considerably slower does not mean that they are not comprehended at all. For this, better tests measuring the products of comprehension processes have to be developed. With the empirical data presented in this article, I have to assume that optimised texts (and also portions of text) are read faster – if this is also associated with a better understanding of text content remains to be shown.

References

Bates, Douglas, Martin Maechler, Ben Bolker, Steven Walker, Rune Haubo Bojesen Christensen & Henrik Singmann. 2014. Lme4: Linear mixed-effects models using eigen and s4 [software manual]. R package version 1.1-6. http://cran.r-project.org/web/packages/lme4/index.html.

---

[8] Figures have to be extracted from the plot from Hansen et al. (2006: 35). Raw figures are not available in the text.

Boston, Marisa, John Hale, Reinhold Kliegl, Umesh Patil & Shravan Vasishth. 2008. Parsing costs as predictors of reading difficulty: An evaluation using the Potsdam Sentence Corpus. *The Mind Research Repository (beta)* 2(1). 1–12.

Clifton, Charles, Adrian Staub & Keith Rayner. 2007. Eye movements in reading words and sentences. In Roger P. G. van Gompel, Martin H. Fischer, Wayne S. Murray & Robin L. Hill (eds.), *Eye movements: A window on mind and brain*, 341–371. Amsterdam: Elsevier.

Demberg, Vera & Frank Keller. 2008. Data from eye-tracking corpora as evidence for theories of syntactic processing complexity. *Cognition* 109(2). 193–210.

Eichhoff-Cyrus, Karin M., Gerd Antos & Rüdiger Schulz. 2009. *Wie denken die Deutschen über die Rechts- und Verwaltungssprache? Eine repräsentative Umfrage der Gesellschaft für deutsche Sprache*. Wiesbaden: Gesellschaft für deutsche Sprache.

Eichhoff-Cyrus, Karin M. & Thomas Strobel. 2009. Einstellungen der Justiz zu Rechts-und Verwaltungssprache. Eine Trendumfrage. *Der Sprachdienst* 53(5). 133–151.

Engbert, Ralf, Antje Nuthmann, Eike M. Richter & Reinhold Kliegl. 2005. SWIFT: A dynamical model of saccade generation during reading. *Psychological Review* 112(4). 777–813.

Frank, Stefan L., Irene Fernandez Monsalve, Robin L. Thompson & Gabriella Vigliocco. 2013. Reading time data for evaluating broad-coverage models of English sentence processing. *Behavior Research Methods* 45(4). 1182–1190.

Hansen, Sandra, Ralph Dirksen, Martin Küchler, Kerstin Kunz & Stella Neumann. 2006. Comprehensible legal texts-utopia or a question of wording? On processing rephrased German court decisions. *Hermes* 36. 15–40.

Hansen-Schirra, Silvia & Stella Neumann. 2004. Linguistische Verständlichmachung in der juristischen Realität. In Kent D. Lerch (ed.), *Recht verstehen. Verständlichkeit, Missverständlichkeit und Unverständlichkeit von Recht*, 167–184. Berlin: de Gruyter.

Hyönä, Jukka, Robert F. Lorch & Mike Rinck. 2003. Eye movement measures to study global text processing. *The mind's eye: Cognitive and applied aspects of eye movement research*. Jukka Hyönä, Ralph Radach & Heiner Deubel (eds.). 313–334.

Jaeger, T. Florian. 2008. Categorical data analysis: Away from ANOVAs (transformation or not) and towards logit mixed models. *Journal of Memory and Language* 59(4). 434–446.

Kennedy, Alan. 2003. The dundee corpus. [CD-ROM]. School of Psychology, The University of Dundee.

Kliegl, Reinhold, Antje Nuthmann & Ralf Engbert. 2006. Tracking the mind during reading: The influence of past, present, and future words on fixation durations. *Journal of Experimental Psychology: General* 135(1). 12–35.

Kliegl, Reinhold, Ellen Grabner, Martin Rolfs & Ralf Engbert. 2004. Length, frequency, and predictability effects of words on eye movements in reading. *European Journal of Cognitive Psychology* 16(1-2). 262–284.

Müller-Feldmeth, Daniel, Sascha Wolfer & Lars Konieczny. 2013. The influence of pre-verbal referents on verb processing: Evidence for similarity-based interference from a new German reading corpus. In C. Frenck-Mestre, F.-X. Alario, N. Nguyen, P. Blache & C. Meunier (eds.), *Proceedings of the 19th Conference on Architectures and Mechanisms for Language Processing (AMLaP)*, 263–287. Berlin: Frank & Timme.

Oksaar, Els. 1988. *Fachsprachliche Dimensionen.* Vol. 4. Tübingen: Gunter Narr.

Patil, Umesh, Shravan Vasishth & Reinhold Kliegl. 2009. Compound effect of probabilistic disambiguation and memory retrievals on sentence processing: Evidence from an eyetracking corpus. In Andrew Howes, David Peebles & Richard Cooper (eds.), *Proceedings of 9th international conference on cognitive modeling*, 92–97. http://eprints.hud.ac.uk/10530/, accessed 2017-07-26.

Plaehn, Oliver. 1998. Annotate Programm-Dokumentation (negra project report). Saarbrücken. http://www.coli.uni-saarland.de/projects/sfb378/negra-corpus/annotate-manual.ps.gz, accessed 2015-10-21.

Pynte, Joel, Boris New & Alan Kennedy. 2008. A multiple regression analysis of syntactic and semantic influences in reading normal text. *Journal of Eye Movement Research* 2(1). 1–11.

R Core Team. 2014. *A language and environment for statistical computing [software manual].* http://www.r-project.org, accessed 2016-07-18.

Rayner, Keith & Alexander Pollatsek. 2006. Eye movement control in reading. In Matthew J. Traxler & Morton A. Gernsbacher (eds.), *Handbook of Psycholinguistics. 2nd edn.* 613–657. Amsterdam: Elsevier.

Reichle, Erik D., Keith Rayner & Alexander Pollatsek. 2003. The EZ reader model of eye-movement control in reading: Comparisons to other models. *Behavioral and Brain Sciences* 26(4). 477–526.

Towfigh, Emanuel Vahid. 2009. Komplexität und Normenklarheit – oder: Gesetze sind für Juristen gemacht. *Der Staat* 1(48). 29–73.

Wagner, Hildegard. 1981. *Die deutsche Verwaltungssprache der Gegenwart:Eine Untersuchung der sprachlichen Sonderform und ihrer Leistung.* 3rd edn. (Schriften des Instituts für deutsche Sprache 9). Düsseldorf: Schwann.

White, Sarah J. 2008. Eye movement control during reading: Effects of word frequency and orthographic familiarity. *Journal of Experimental Psychology: Human Perception and Performance* 34(1). 205–223.

Wolfer, Sascha, Daniel Müller-Feldmeth, Lars Konieczny, Uli Held, Karin Maksymski, Silvia Hansen-Schirra, Sandra Hansen & Peter Auer. 2013. PopSci: A reading corpus of popular science texts with rich multi-level annotations. A case study. In *Book of abstracts of the 17th European Conference on Eye Movements.* Lund.

Name index

Subject index

www.ingramcontent.com/pod-product-compliance
Lightning Source LLC
LaVergne TN
LVHW082033050326
832904LV00006B/274